THE UNIVERSITY OF MICHIGAN
CENTER FOR JAPANESE STUDIES

MICHIGAN PAPERS IN JAPANESE STUDIES
NO. 1

POLITICAL LEADERSHIP IN CONTEMPORARY JAPAN

edited by

Terry Edward MacDougall

Ann Arbor

Center for Japanese Studies
The University of Michigan

1982

ISBN 0-939512-06-8

Copyright © 1982

by

Center for Japanese Studies
The University of Michigan

Library of Congress Cataloging in Publication Data

Political leadership in contemporary Japan.

(Michigan papers in Japanese studies; no. 1)
Includes bibliographies.
1. Political parties—Japan. 2. Politicians—
Japan. 3. Leadership. 4. Japan—Politics and
government—1945- . I. MacDougall, Terry Edward,
1941- . II. University of Michigan. Center for
Japanese Studies. III. Series.
JQ1698.A1P64 1982   324.252   82-9634
ISBN 0-939512-06-8

Printed in the United States of America

TABLE OF CONTENTS

Introduction

Those who do not read Japanese seldom have access to analytic studies of the fascinating and surprisingly diverse world of contemporary Japanese political leadership. This little volume hardly fills that gap, but it does constitute a step toward bringing to the English reader some sense of the norms, beliefs, styles, and modes of exercising power of Japanese political leaders and the organizational and political contexts which are changing leadership role expectations. A second volume in this series concentrates more explicitly on leadership recruitment, although the subject is also addressed here.[1]

All of the essays in this volume highlight specific politicians, while attempting to develop analytic categories to understand the broader significance of these types of leaders. Included are the following: a Liberal Democratic Party prime minister and faction leader (Fukuda Takeo) who rose "almost effortlessly" to the pinnacle of power on the basis of an elitist educational and bureaucratic career background and another (Tanaka Kakuei) who took advantage of the chaotic wartime and immediate postwar period to overcome the limitations of his commoner background by developing an entrepreneurial style that makes him even today "the most powerful man in Japan"; a younger conservative leader (Kōno Yōhei) who, with certain others of his generation, found life within the restrictive but predictable career paths of the ruling Liberal Democrats less attractive than the risky option of forming his own New Liberal Club; an unconventional Socialist chairman (Asukata Ichio) who bucks the pull toward coalition making among the opposition parties in favor of his belief that this major but perpetual opposition party must first reconstruct itself and structure a new popular consensus that can legitimize a coalitional alternative to the Liberal Democrats; parliamentary leaders (like lower-house speaker Maeo Shigesaburō, directors of the House Management Committee, and heads of the Diet policy committees of the various parties) who are projected into increasingly influential roles by changing electorial trends and popular expectations; an innovative and dynamic mayor (Suzuki Heizaburō) who, taking advantage of the considerable authority afforded by Japan's "presidential" system of local chief executives, pursues his own priorities, mobilizing the requisite support despite the lack of national guidance and the

---

1. John Creighton Campbell, ed., *Parties, Candidates, and Voters in Japan: Six Quantitative Studies.* Michigan Papers in Japanese Studies 2.

opposition of former backers; and the "power behind the throne" (Matsunaga Yasuzaemon and Komori Takeshi) whose visions move prime ministers and governors as well as their own followers in powerful public and private bureaucracies.

Kent Calder, through a systematic comparison of former prime ministers Fukuda Takeo and Tanaka Kakuei, contrasts two predominant types of postwar, conservative political leaders, the *kanryō* (bureaucrat) and the *shomin* (commoner). Both are "political brokers" (persons providing private-sector groups and individuals special access to direct material benefits or regulatory actions dispensed by official bureaucracy) rather than originators or legitimizers of policy.[2] Calder stresses that the high frequency of political brokers among Japanese conservative leaders is facilitated not simply by a cultural predilection to make decisions outside public view, where conflicts are more easily mediated, but also by the character of one-party dominance during an era of rapid economic growth, which created abundant resources to broker for a demanding public.

Contrasting Fukuda and Tanaka (the archetypical *kanryō* and *shomin*, respectively), Calder demonstrates why the former high-level bureaucrat turned conservative politician has had a relatively easier task playing the political broker role; his prestigeous educational background (Tokyo University's Faculty of Law) and seniority within officialdom provide him with easy access to the ministries and abundant opportunities to influence the career chances of rising bureaucrats, who are themselves in a strong position to allocate credit, licenses, regulatory decisions, and other resources desired by the private sector. By contrast, the *shomin*, if he is to be a successful political broker, must be more entrepreneurial in style, creating resources (like new postcareer jobs or party nominations for ex-bureaucrats and special credit facilities for private groups) to construct his institutional ties to the establishment and develop private clienteles.

The prevalence of political brokers at the helm of the ruling Liberal Democrats, Calder suggests, has had a telling impact on the country's political economy, giving it an expansionary thrust and complicating bureaucratic control. But, in turn, the slower rates of economic growth following disturbances in the international economic system in the 1970s may impell a new content to conservative brokerage. Brokers in an "era of scarcity" may have to appeal to such nonacquisitive sentiments as nationalism or a desire for a just society. Importantly, this transition to a new, not yet clearly defined, conservative style of leadership coincides with the impending rise of a new generation of conservative leaders.

2. The line between legitimate brokerage and political corruption is ill defined in many societies. Calder's listing of Tanaka's record of brokerage dramatically illustrates this in the Japanese case.

Susan Pharr's essay focuses on the question of status conflict inherent in the clear demarcation of political generation and hierarchically defined allocation of rewards within Japanese conservative political circles. Noting that within the Liberal Democratic Party political age (numbers of times elected to the National Diet) and biological age largely determine the status hierarchy, which may be adjusted but not restructured by performance criteria, Pharr delineates the enormous resources (government, parliamentary and party posts, election nominations and campaign funds, policy choices, etc.) in the hands of Liberal Democratic power brokers (largely, former prime ministers and heads of factions). Followers from seceding generations have little recourse but patiently to learn the rules of the game as they await the calling of their numbers for higher and higher levels of power and authority. The inequality inherent in this hierarchical arrangement of power, which permeates all sorts of Japanese organizations, has been made more salient and difficult for younger generations to bear as postwar equalitarian values become more firmly internalized. Yet a fundamental dilemma remains for the party and Japanese society, since few channels exist for working out such status-based conflicts.

Pharr documents the convoluted process by which such an intergenerational conflict within the Liberal Democratic Party led Kōno Yōhei and several others of junior rank to bolt the party in 1976 to form the New Liberal Club. Meticuluously tracing five analytically distinguishable stages of conflict behavior, she identifies the origin of the conflict, the declining incentives of young (as opposed to middle-level or older) conservatives to abide by traditional hierarchy, and why this particular group rather than some other had the wherewithal to expect something better outside the governing party. Before reaching that final stage, however, she shows how the very hierarchical structure of power shaped the only possible hope for renegotiating the terms of status within the party—by seeking the mediation of a middle generation of conservative leaders, some of them impatient for top leadership themselves.

My essay on Asukata Ichio, chairman of the Japan Socialist Party, contrasts sharply with the earlier two chapters because Socialist leaders command few of the resources available to the party in power and, moreover, find themselves in the midst of a historical predicament. In short, perpetual opposition has contributed to the maintenance of a revolutionary rhetoric and ideological line entirely out of synchronization with the party's moderate activities as an established and often effective participant in Japan's thriving parliamentary system. The leftists fear that moderation in principle (revisionism) might diminish the party's ability to check conservative departures from postwar constitutional tenets impedes a resolution of this classical socialist predicament of reconciling principle with practice in a capitalist democracy. The paralysis of the party is as much a consequence of this fundamental predicament as of its many specific problems. Starting with the assumption that the beliefs and abilities of political leaders make a difference in the resolution of such questions, I have focused the essay on Asukata's approach to two dilemmas rooted in the historical predicament—first, the leadership dilemma of how to close the gap between the formal role of the chairman as "party leader" and his very limited power in practice and, second, the internal-external dilemma of how to maintain party cohesion and strength while pursuing a coalitional strategy.

During his first term as chairman (1977-79), Asukata devoted his major efforts to achieving party cohesion. While seeking to heal old wounds—the party almost split in 1977—by a collective effort to build "a party of one million," frame detailed policy positions, and bring fresh blood and ideas into the party, Asukata tried to avoid making a choice for coalition with the centrist parties, which was urged upon him by Socialist moderates, labor leaders, and a critical press. Instead, I have argued that he pursued a "mass strategy" of bypassing a party-based coalitional choice until a popular legitimacy could be established for an alternative to Liberal Democratic Party rule. Asukata's position was rooted not only in his desire to manage the leftist-moderate split within party ranks (as was argued by the press) but also in his evaluation of the strength of the conservative establishment and belief that fundamental political change requires a mass base. Asukata failed to convince the party's collective leadership of the efficacy of this strategy because it seemed excessively slow given the flux of Japanese politics and because as a quasi outsider (having spent the past fifteen years as mayor of Yokohama), Asukata lacked a large, devoted followership at the center to communicate his intentions and bargain effectively for the acceptance of his position. Nonetheless, in a low-keyed manner he has brought the party to the juncture of addressing its historical predicament, not by a fullscale revisionism but by a choice for an open-ended socialism based on Japanese realities. Whether this choice, if fully adopted through a revision of "The Road to Socialism in Japan," will be enough and on time to meet voter concerns remains to be seen.

Asukata, then, has provided neither the "transformative" leadership of an Eda Saburō bent on fullscale revisionism nor the "managerial" leadership of a Narita Tomomi, but rather a mass-oriented, reformist leadership which seeks party strength and renovation through its grasp of the realities of Japanese capitalism and its involvement in shaping a new mass consensus for reformist policies and a coalitional alternative compatible with Socialist ideals.

Ellis Krauss' study of changing leadership roles and role conflicts in Japan's Parliament focuses on the partisan-accomodation dilemma—i.e., how parliamentary leaders reconcile their partisan interests with parliamentary goals. Krauss begins by assessing the organizational context of Japanese legislative behavior, placing it along the comparative continuum between an "arena" model and a "transformative" model of legislatures. In the former, partisan goals are paramount and parliamentary leaders have little autonomy from party leadership;   in the latter, powerful parliamentary leaders emerge to accommodate differences among the parties.   Despite efforts by the Allied Occupation to introduce a functionally organized committee system and strong speakers and committee chairmen (i.e., an American "transformative" legislature), Krauss argues that in the 1950s and 1960s the Japanese Diet was largely an arena-type legislature.   The perpetual rule of the Liberal Democrats left little incentive for government or opposition leaders to place accommodative strategies above partisan ones.   Parliamentary leaders like the speaker, committee chairmen, and Diet strategy specialists had little independent authority and would have to yield to party executives, who might prefer parliamentary confrontation to public accommodation not only on matters of ideological principle but also of constituency interest.   Although the latter type of issues were often negotiated behind the scenes by the Liberal Democrats and Socialists in the 1960s, strong partisan interests kept such behavior out of the public arena.

Krauss argues that this situation changed dramatically in the 1970s because of several factors including (1)   the longterm decline of the two established parties, creating a multiparty system and, eventually, an era of "equally balanced forces" between government and opposition, (2)   the enhanced importance of the Diet's committee system, no longer wholly controlled by the party in power, and the need for all parties to consider how their parliamentary strategies might influence coalitional chances, and (3)   public demand for cleaner, more open politics and concern for new issues that cut across old left-right divisions.   The result has been changed leadership role norms, giving greater prominence to those with skills at interparty accommodation.

Drawing upon his intensive elite interviews as well as data on career patterns among Japanese Diet members, Krauss demonstrates several key consequences of these changes: (1) Party leaders were under strong pressure to reconcile partisan interests with interparty accommodation within the Diet; (2) Parliamentary leaders had greater political experience and increasingly were being recruited to influential government and party posts; and (3) Parliamentary leaders acquired more autonomy and authority vis-a-vis party leaders. Thus, the political process in Japan by the late 1970s was far more complex than in the past, involved many more actors, and was played out more often within the National Diet.

Ronald Aqua's essay on mayoral leadership in Japan, which draws on the author's survey of thirty-seven medium-sized cities as well as a more in-depth analysis of Mitaka City in Tokyo, presents a picture of forceful, innovative leadership at the local level. It is a useful antidote to the cultural explanations of Japanese leadership as necessarily consensus seeking and to the notion that local leaders passively reflect the priorities of higher levels of the administrative system.   Aqua describes how Mayor Suzuki Heizaburō began his administration with a clear set of priorities, based on his professional training in public health and socialist leanings, and pursued them to a successful conclusion despite the initial lack of national assistance and resistance from some of his original partisan supporters. He attributes such examples of local priority setting by city mayors to two factors. First, as Krauss emphasizes in his essay, institutional or organizational context makes a difference. Japan's directly elected mayors (and governors) have "presidential" powers and are not merely "first among equals" as are factional leaders of the two major national parties. (Interestingly, as pointed out in my essay, when Asukata Ichio set his conditions for accepting the chairmanship of the Japan Socialist Party, he sought to strengthen the institutional context of that post by giving it a broad (all-party) electoral base of legitimacy such as he enjoyed as mayor of Yokohama.) Aqua's second factor in explaining mayoral leadership is the individual's style and political beliefs. Thus, the informed, visible, and even aggressive style of many Japanese mayors may be related not simply to the institutional context but to such recruitment characteristics as their strong local roots, high educational attainments, and long experience in prominent administrative or professional roles, which provide them with a basis for establishing their priorities separately from those of the parties or national administration.

Richard Samuels' study of "Power Behind the Throne" offers new insights into an important, if little acknowledged, type of political leadership in Japan—that which is exercised by powerful figures without official bureaucratic or political roles. Intriguingly, the processes of developing real political influence that Samuels analyzes in the cases of Matsunaga Yasuzaemon (a conservative boss) and Komori Takeshi (a progressive one) are strikingly parallel to Calder's analysis of brokerage by top-ranked, Liberal Democratic leaders. Both authors stress that consensual norms often force leaders behind the scenes where, far from the din of press and public, they engage in the protracted conflict-reducing process of *nemawashi* or extensive consultation. If this norm impells leading Liberal Democratic Party politicians to maneuver and broker resources behind the scenes, it also projects powerful private figures into similar roles. As in the case of politicians, they too must have wide contacts within public and private bureaucracies and independent resources if they are to function effectively.

What is most striking about Samuels' analysis is the similarity between the way the conservative boss, Matsunaga, and the progressive one, Komori, exercise their power. Their power is not "informal"—based merely on strong personal ties with persons in high-ranking public office. It is carefully structured. Both Matsunaga and Komori had "broadly based, well-placed networks of lower-ranking officials throughout a variety of public and private bureaucracies." As their followers, nurtured earlier through the provision of career-enhancing opportunities, moved into positions of policy responsibility, they could be called upon to support the initiatives of the private leaders who remain behind the scenes. The visions of such persons cannot be ignored in trying to understand political leadership in contempory Japan.

Moreover, in noting how the prewar association of postwar progressive boss Komori with Fukuda Takeo, then a rising Finance Ministry bureaucrat, facilitated accommodation between Fukuda as prime minister and Minobe Ryōkichi, the progressive governor of Tokyo through whom Komori operated, Samuels provides a concrete illustration of the "seamless web of elite contacts" which facilitate communication between right and left, ins and outs, in Japanese politics. Similarly, Aqua's analysis of Mayor Suzuki, my own of Mayor and, later, Chairman Asukata, and Krauss' of Diet leadership all suggest means by which seemingly unbridgeable gaps in partisan perspectives are in fact narrowed in practice.

All of the essays in this volume are the product of original research by young American political scientists.[3] In most cases the essays are based on the authors' larger ongoing studies of Japanese political leadership. It is our hope that the essays, by stressing a variety of leadership styles, goals, and skills in specific cases, may not only partially correct the stereotypical view of a uniform managerial style of Japanese political leadership, but also stimulate further, more systematic studies of political leadership in contemporary Japan.

3. The essays by Pharr, Krauss, and myself are revisions of papers originally presented at the Annual Meeting of the Association for Asian Studies, April 23, 1980, Washington, D.C. Aqua's essay appears in essentially the same form as presented at that panel. The essays by Calder and Samuels were written especially for this volume. The members of the original conference panel wish to thank Professor Robert Putnam of Harvard University for his challenging criticisms of the papers.

KANRYŌ VS. *SHOMIN*:
CONTRASTING DYNAMICS OF CONSERVATIVE LEADERSHIP IN POSTWAR JAPAN

Kent E. Calder

One spring day in March 1929, as several hundred members of the Tokyo establishment watched approvingly, young Fukuda Takeo of Gunma Prefecture received the coveted *Gin Dokei* at the command of Emperor Hirohito. Receipt of this silver watch, given to the top-ranking graduate of the elite Tokyo Imperial University Faculty of Law in prewar days, symbolized one's entry into the realms of the best and the brightest. It was a major initial step on the road to leadership in the fixed, elitist society that was prewar Japan.

While Fukuda Takeo was receiving the *Gin Dokei* to the plaudits of the Tokyo establishment, his rival-to-be in the prime ministerial contests of the 1970s, Tanaka Kakuei, was a fifth grader in rural Niigata Prefecture, of impoverished *Ura Nihon* on the Japan Sea coast. In years to come, Tanaka never received a high-school diploma, much less the *Gin Dokei*. While Fukuda was moving predictably from post to post within the elite Ministry of Finance (MOF) in his early professional years, Tanaka was moving erratically from one menial job to another, working successively as day laborer, insurance-firm employee, apprentice journalist, army draftee, and small-scale contractor. Tanaka, who sang *naniwa bushi*, or traditional folk songs, on NHK national radio weeks after taking his first Cabinet post, was the quintessential *shomin*, or commoner, a sharp contrast to the elite *kanryō*, or bureaucrat, Fukuda. Tanaka was also thirteen years Fukuda's junior in a seniority-oriented society, and acquired a reputation as a "computerized bulldozer" in a nation placing great store in slowly and carefully crafted consensus.

Yet, in July 1972 Tanaka was selected over Fukuda to succeed Satō Eisaku as prime minister. Tanaka's proxy, Ōhira Masayoshi, was chosen prime minister over an incumbent Fukuda in December 1978. Tanaka had been elected Dietman at twenty-eight and appointed Cabinet minister at thirty-nine, younger than any of his contemporaries. At fifty-four he became the youngest prime minister modern Japan has ever had. The Japanese political system allowed Tanaka also to

1

maintain preeminent political influence in wide areas of policy and government personnel recruitment even after two arrests and three resignations from high public office because of scandal. Richard Nixon, one could speculate, might have been envious.

The contrasting social origins and ultimate political fates of Tanaka Kakuei and Fukuda Takeo reveal much about the dynamics of conservative leadership in postwar Japan. To analyze these careers in a fashion generating hypotheses about leadership in general which might be tested comparatively, it is useful to ask three basic sets of questions:

(1) How were these leaders recruited? In terms of the specific cases at hand, how did Fukuda and Tanaka happen to rise to leadership positions within the postwar political order?
(2) What function did the leaders in question actually perform within the political system? Were they legitimators, originators, or brokers among preexisting interests? Why did they assume a given function at a particular point in time?
(3) What are the consequences of the particular patterns of leadership exhibited by these men for the larger econo-political systems within which leadership takes place?

The Elite Route and the Entrepreneurial Route to Leadership Status

Through. Japanese political history, there has been a pronounced bias toward conservatism in pe........ .....ruitment. For over one thousand years, from even before the days of the Fujiwara, there has been a strong .... for leaders to be succeeded by relatives or former close associates and for self-perpetuating establishments to develop and persist. This pattern, while observable to some degree world-wide, seems especially pronounced in Japan, particularly in comparison to developments in North American frontier societies such as the United States.

While conservative leaders have generally perpetuated themselves and their associates with unusual consistency in Japan, there has been a recurring pattern of periodic shocks to the established order, throwing hierarchical relations into turmoil and allowing leaders of new backgrounds to rise. During the late Muromachi period, and the fluid *sengoku jidai* following (late sixteenth century), leaders of peasant origin such as Hideyoshi Toyotomi rose to contend with those of higher social backgrounds such as Oda Nobunaga. The early Meiji era (1868 to perhaps 1880) was to some extent another such period.

Contemporary Japanese have compared the lawlessness and absence of coherent leadership during the *sengoku* period with the difficulties the ruling

Liberal Democratic Party (LDP) had in providing leadership in the 1970s, especially during its temporary loss of a stable majority in the Diet between December 1976 and June 1980. (See Krauss, this volume.) But a more appropriate parallel with the *sengoku jidai* is the 1941-1955 period. Despite the persistence and even increase in the influence of the conservative bureaucracy during the 1940s that Chalmers Johnson, John Dower, and others observe, the chaos of war and the subsequent purge, land reform, and *zaibatsu* dissolution induced temporary fluidity in existing leadership hierarchies. New institutions and new types of leaders had a brief chance to rise, profoundly affecting the dynamics of conservative leadership ever since.

This chaotic era was the period when the contrasting careers of Tanaka Kakuei and Fukuda Takeo got underway. When Imperial Navy planes attacked Pearl Harbor on December 8, 1941 (Tokyo Standard Time), Fukuda had just left his post as budget examiner for the Army Ministry to become financial advisor to the collaborationist regime in Nanking. At war's end he was bureau chief in the MOF Secretariat, and by 1947 chief of the Budget Bureau; he was clearly a candidate for MOF *jimujikan* (administrative vice minister), the most coveted bureaucratic position in Japan. In 1950, Fukuda was arrested in the Shōwa Denkō scandal (for receiving a bribe of ¥350,000), and forced to resign from the Ministry of Finance without becoming vice minister. But he was nevertheless able, two years later, to garner a Diet seat on the basis of his almost impeccable bureaucratic credentials. *Gin Dokei* recipient Fukuda progressed with equal rapidity under both Tōjō and MacArthur, and his professional career proceeded untouched by the chaos around him. That career epitomized the continuity which was one major dimension of Japanese life during the turbulent 1940s.

For Tanaka, on the other hand, the coming of war had profound career implications. In 1939 he was drafted into the Imperial Army and sent to Manchuria. By Pearl Harbor Day, he had been released from military service, after a near-fatal bout of pneumonia, and had returned to a menial part-time, construction-industry job in Niigata while trying to regain his strength. Within four years, however, his economic standing had been strikingly transformed. Tanaka had become a prosperous contractor, reputedly wealthy mainly from largesse gathered through entrepreneurial activities in Korea at war's end (Tachibana 1976a:149-59). And in 1947, when Fukuda assumed directorship of the MOF Budget Bureau, Tanaka became a Dietman, at only twenty-eight years of age.

Two incidents transformed Tanaka's prospects. In 1942 he married the daughter of a Niigata contractor with numerous contacts in the Home Ministry, Army Ministry, and other agencies rapidly expanding their construction activities under the demands of wartime. In 1944, largely as a result of his father-in-law's contacts, the twenty-six-year-old Tanaka landed a major army contract for relocating a piston-ring plant from Oji, Japan, to Taejon, Korea, to render it less vulnerable to allied bombing. In 1980 yen, the contract was worth ¥9-10 billion, or around $50 million (Tachibana 1976a:150).

Tanaka was given a sizeable advance by the army to undertake the relocation of the piston-ring plant, and went to Korea in early 1945 to plan the logistics of the undertaking. But in the chaos of war's end, the project was never completed, and a final accounting for the funds Tanaka received was never made. In his autobiography, Tanaka explains ambiguously that the project resources at his command were used "for the good of the new Korea" (Tanaka 1966:170-71). But it appears likely that a substantial portion of the army funds were appropriated by Tanaka and used to launch his political career (Tachibana 1976a:154-68). Shortly after war's end, Tanaka, in any case, became a significant financial benefactor of the new Progressive Party (*Shimpo Tō*) headed by Machida Chūji and in 1947 financed his own successful campaign for the Diet.

War and reconstruction exerted a profound influence on the dynamics of conservative leadership in Japan that greatly transcends the case of Tanaka Kakuei. They weakened many of the mainline establishment groups, such as the major *zaibatsu*. Wartime profiteering created vast pools of hoarded wealth in a largely impoverished land and new loci of political power, often operating mostly behind the scenes. Kodama Yoshio, made wealthy by trafficking in precious stones and contraband as a procurement agent for the Japanese Imperial Army in China, rose to political influence in conservative ranks as a result of the war. In the early postwar years he is reported to have provided at times well over half the total campaign funding for Yoshida Shigeru and Satō Eisaku's Liberal Party. Kishi Nobusuke, Minister of Munitions in Tōjō's Cabinet and coordinator of the *Sangyō Setsubi Eidan* (Industrial Equipment Corporation) in the latter stages of the war, is said to have profited substantiallly from the dispersal of military raw material stocks, enriching himself sufficiently to support his political career. Kodama, Kishi, and Tanaka were three of the most important financial pillars and power brokers in conservative ranks throughout the postwar period, and all gained a financial base for their political operations during World War II and the period immediately following.

Wartime chaos and its aftermath, then, greatly aided Tanaka Kakuei in his early career, but did little to promote the advancement of Fukuda Takeo inside the bureaucracy. Why these two individuals advanced steadily (after their debuts as freshmen Dietmen—Tanaka in 1947 and Fukuda in 1952) can be answered by looking at the roles they played in the overall Japanese political system.

Conservative Politicians as Resource Brokers

Leaders (both formal and informal) can be seen as having at least three major functional roles in relation to policy formation—legitimizing particular patterns of policy, originating policy positions, and brokering preexisting demands for some form of policy output. The frequency with which leaders perform one or another of these functions varies significantly from nation to nation, with legitimation and brokerage particularly pronounced in Japan.

A cultural predisposition to settle major issues of policy in private through intermediaries, and in public only to ratify, rather than to decide, policy questions may account for the frequency with which formal leaders appear as legitimators rather than as originators of policy in Japan. (Some formal leaders, such as the emperor and many elderly corporate presidents, act exclusively as legitimators, participating in decision making only ceremonially to ratify decisions which have already been made.) However, structural characteristics of the Japanese political economy appear most important in explaining why Japanese conservative leaders function so frequently as brokers and why ability at brokerage has been such an important precondition for success in modern Japanese politics.

In this paper, "brokerage" is understood to mean the act of mediating between private-sector groups or individuals desiring direct material benefits or regulatory actions conferring such benefits, on the one hand, and governmental bodies perceived capable of providing such services, on the other. The mediation of more abstract demands for "national security," "clean government," "crime control," and other public goods is not construed as brokerage, nor are nonmediatory policy initiatives by public figures themselves. The heart of brokerage as considered here is the mediating role of politicians in "pork-barrel politics." "Brokerage" can be thought of as a major subcategory within the broader classification which Theodore Lowi calls "distributive" policy making (Lowi 1972:299-300).

Every nation, of course, has its "smoke-filled rooms" where political intermediaries hammer out patterns of compensation for private-sector clients. What is distinctive about Japanese politics is that brokerage is a major part of total political activity, and central ability at brokerage determines who leads the nation. In sharp contrast to Europe, and to a lesser degree the United States, basic ideologically oriented debates on the proper nature of the domestic political system and of class relationships do not rend the Japanese political order, nor are foreign-policy controversies high on the political agenda. Public-works expenditures, allocation of government land, and the distribution of subsidies for farmers, small business, and so on are the questions which agitate Japanese politicians, especially those in conservative ranks. The salience of brokerage-related, "pork-barrel" politics is clear from the composition of the national budget. Subsidies comprised a percentage of the whole much higher than the average for the OECD over the two decades 1955-1975, and public works expenditures were also unusually high.

The correlation between brokerage skills and tenure in national leadership positions also appears unusually strong in Japan, suggesting the importance of brokerage abilities in determining who leads the nation. Of the eight United States presidents since Franklin D. Roosevelt, only three (Lyndon Johnson, Richard Nixon, and Gerald Ford) had extensive brokerage experience in national politics before being elected chief executive. Of the remaining five nonprofessional politicians, one was a former general, another a former actor, and the third a former peanut farmer. France has routinely elected aristocratic presidents like Charles de Gaulle and Valery Giscard d'Estaing, who disdain the political process and who are relative newcomers to its intricacies. Even parliamentary democracies like Britain frequently place higher priority on policy orientation than on brokerage skills in selecting leadership, as the selection of figures such as Margaret Thatcher, Edward Heath, and Winston Churchill to head the Conservative Party suggest. In Japan, however, factors other than brokerage skill (ideological orientation, charisma, rhetorical skill, and so on) have been relatively unimportant to leadership success.

Brokerage ability in Japan derives preeminently from stable, institutionalized ties with the bureaucracy which allow a politician to consistently deliver resources formally controlled by government ministries (such as budget allocations and construction permits) into the hands of private-sector groups. Former bureaucrats, with a wealth of personal contacts developed from years of government service, tend to be best able to mediate for private-sector groups. Not surprisingly, such former officials (including Yoshida Shigeru, Kishi Nobusuke, Ikeda Hayato, Satō Eisaku, Fukuda Takeo, and Ōhira Masayoshi) served as prime minister for over 80 percent of the period 1952-1980. Such nonbureaucrats as have served were mostly either compromise candidates like Suzuki Zenkō, who possessed their own intraparty mediating skills, or leaders like Tanaka Kakuei, who developed institutionalized ties with the bureaucracy like those the former officials already possessed. Practically the only common distinguishing trait of all postwar Japanese prime ministers is that they have been first and foremost skilled brokers of some variety.

The central factor forcing conservative Japanese politicians into brokerage roles has been the tradition of a strong central bureaucracy capable of profoundly affecting the livelihood of citizens. This reality, combined with the uneven responsiveness of the bureaucracy to demands from various sectors of the population, has caused some interest groups to rely on party politicians, often with bureaucratic origins, to satisfy their demands. Following the Meiji restoration, for example, bureaucrats allocated budget funds preferentially to areas such as southern Kyushu and western Honshu which had spearheaded the restoration and from which the bureaucrats themselves came. Other regions, such as Tōhoku in the northeast, felt deprived and allied with party politicians to seek compensation. Not surprisingly, the leading political broker of prewar Japan,

Hara Kei, was a native of Fukushima Prefecture in the northeast, an area (within the Mito domain) which had supported the Tokugawa Shogunate. Through extensive brokerage activities during ten years as Home Minister—particularly in providing railroads to outlying areas not favored by the bureaucracy—Hara ultimately rose to the prime ministership in 1918, the first party politician to do so. (For further details on Hara Kei, see Najita 1967.)

Although Hara Kei himself was clearly a great political broker and rose to the prime ministership on his skills in that area, brokerage was still not normally performed as extensively by politicians, nor was it as central to their success, as was to be the case after World War II. Brokerage became more crucial in conservative politics, and success at brokerage a more important determinant of political success for conservative politicians, for the following reasons:

(1) Reestablishment of a multiparty democracy, which made politicians more vulnerable to demands by constituents for brokerage services.

(2) Continuous one-party rule for more than a generation from 1955. The increasingly institutionalized relationship between bureaucrats and the LDP makes it relatively simple for politicians to call on the services of bureaucrats and increases conservative politicians' influence on the inner workings of the bureaucracy.

(3) Rapid economic growth within a highly regulated political system. The headlong economic growth of the 1950s, 1960s, and early 1970s created imbalances between supply and demand (for credit and raw materials, for example) which had to be brokered whenever the bureaucracy refused to let the market work, as it did frequently.

Rapid growth promoted brokerage in several ways. It transformed population distribution and industrial structures, creating conflicts between regulatory patterns and economic realities that needed to be brokered. For example, population during the 1960s grew rapidly in certain prefectures around metropolitan Tokyo, such as Saitama and Chiba. These areas needed more bank branches, for which authorization was controlled by the Ministry of Finance. LDP politicians, especially those with MOF backgrounds, were often enlisted as brokers to lobby for new branch authorizations. Pressure for political brokerage also developed in the transportation industry—increased numbers of taxis and expanded airline networks had to be authorized, for example. Points of tension between business and regulation are natural sites for political brokerage, and they were numerous in the Japan of the 1950s, 1960s, and 1970s. This was because these decades were a period of extraordinarily rapid growth and social transformation, supervised by a powerful bureaucracy which found changes in its accustomed formal modes of operation unpleasant and difficult.

Perhaps the most important consequence of rapid growth for patterns of political brokerage in Japan was that the resources available to the state for allocation increased: between 1955 and 1978 net government expenditures increased more than thirtyfold, from ¥2.7 trillion to ¥96.7 trillion (Nihon Ginkō 1979:210).   The proportion composed by the politically strategic, public-works expenditures (for roads, bridges, ports, and so on) was rising also: in 1934-1936, public works comprised 7.5 percent of the central government's general account budget; in 1955, 10 percent; in fiscal 1979, 17.5 percent (Ōkurashō 1979:274). Grants in aid to local government, some of which comprise a highly politicized resource, rose from 0.3 percent of the national budget in 1934-1936 to 15.5 percent of a massively larger budget in 1979 (Ōkurashō 1979:274).

Rapid growth also helped increase the value of government lands, which are sold to the public by the Ministry of Finance in an often highly politicized process. The increasing international competitiveness and trade surpluses that accompanied growth also created, at times, a demand for emergency import programs which were often politicized and naturally involved substantial brokerage by politicians. Foreign aid contracts, which began to multiply rapidly during the 1970s, have also become a major resource brokered by politicians— particularly large aid contracts subsidizing trade with the People's Republic of China.

Given the pressures on Japanese conservative politicians during the 1950s and 1960s to become resource brokers, and the rapidly expanding volume of resources to be allocated, it is not surprising that skills at allocating existing resources, and even at creating new resources to allocate, were a key factor in the political rise of Tanaka Kakuei and, to a lesser degree, of Fukuda Takeo. Fukuda's brokerage has involved allocating loans, budget quotas, and certain regulatory benefits bestowed by the Ministry of Finance, where he served as a bureaucrat for over twenty years and as minister for a total of four and one-half years between 1965 and 1974. Tanaka's brokerage activities have been mainly in the construction, transportation, and broadcasting sectors, and only secondarily in finance. Fukuda's brokerage style is somewhat less direct than Tanaka's; he is said to work more through intermediaries, such as former MOF *kobun* (junior associate) Sumita Satoshi, and son-in-law Ochi Michio. (During Fukuda's prime ministership there were, however, important nonbrokerage issues of policy, such as the 7 percent growth issue in 1977-1978, on which he directly and personally asserted himself.)

Despite differences of style and area of policy concern, Tanaka and Fukuda faced the strategic problem of all Japanese political brokers: establishing a consistent capability to deliver resources formally controlled by the bureaucracy (budget allocations, construction permits, approvals of bank merger applications, and so on) into the hands of private-sector interest groups. The solution to this

salaries, perquisites, and retirement benefits for the ex-bureaucrats who join them. During the two years that Tanaka was prime minister, for example, salaries of public corporation chairmen (almost all of them former bureaucrats) jumped 67 percent, from an average of ¥480,000/ month to ¥800,000/month (Seirōkyō Chōsa Honbu 1979:77). In 1974 Prime Minister Tanaka Kakuei secured Diet approval to establish the Chiiki Shinkō Seibi Kōdan (Regional Promotion Facilities Corporation). This public corporation had the largest complement of ex-bureaucrats (sixteen—five from Transport, four from Construction, and three from Finance) of all public corporations in Japan at the time of its formation.

(2) Support for the political aspirations of top bureaucrats. Of the ten former bureaucrats elected in the national constituency in the June 1980 upper-house election, for example, four were Tanaka supporters, including two former Vice Ministers of Construction, one Vice Minister of Finance, and one Vice Minister of Agriculture (*Nihon Keizai Shimbun*, June 25, 1980). A typical case was that of former MOF Vice Minister Hatoyama Iichirō, who, together with his MOF contemporaries, had made Tanaka an honorary member of their *dōki-kai* (entering class association). Tanaka's brokerage insured critical electoral support from several small Buddhist religious groups he had aided in the late 1960s on behalf of Hatoyama, an elite MOF bureaucrat who had had no previous connection to those groups.

(3) Aid in sustaining within the Diet policy positions advocated by bureaucrats. During 1968-1969, for example, when Tanaka was chairman of the LDP Rice Price Committee, he is said to have cooperated with MOF bureaucrats in moderating producer rice-price increases. One of the most attractive features of Tanaka Kakuei, in the view of Japanese bureaucrats, is his dependability, stemming from his ability to deliver on promises made.

Although Tanaka and Fukuda both cultivated close relations with the bureaucracy, their brokerage activities have been rather different. Fukuda, with his establishment credentials, succeeded in most cases despite a diffident, low-key, and often passive approach to nonbureaucrats, waiting for private groups to come to him or his representatives with problems to solve. Fukuda has been able to concentrate, in his intraparty activities, on policy definition (rather than on political organization) in the fashion of the classic eighteenth- and nineteenth-century British statesmen. Aside from his four and one-half years as MOF minister, Fukuda has spent more time as chairman of the LDP's Policy Affairs Research Council (*Seichō Kai*) than in any other political position.

Tanaka Kakuei, by contrast, has been forced by his lowly origins to aggressively "sell *on*" (i.e., to place others in his debt by seeking to do them favors). His brokerage has consisted not so much of passively mediating among contending positions, or in formulating abstract policy, as in giving and demanding favors in a continuous stream of discrete transactions. Tanaka's major intraparty activity, which aided him mightily in gaining the prime ministership, was more than four years' service as LDP secretary general.

Examples which illustrate the dynamics of Tanaka's brokerage include the following:

(1) Allocation of government land. While MOF minister during 1962–1965, Tanaka "sold on" in the form of choice national lands (*koku yūchi*) to large numbers of major construction companies and manufacturing firms. Tachibana estimates that during Tanaka's three-year term at MOF he sold as much government land to the private sector as all the other MOF ministers during the 1957–1971 period combined (Tachibana 1976:75). During this period Tanaka offered first-rate, central-Tokyo parcels of government land to all three major Tokyo-based dailies—the *Yomiuri Shimbun*, *Asahi Shimbun*, and *Nihon Keizai Shimbun*. They all accepted, and have been remarkably conciliatory for most of the period since. In 1966 the *Nihon Keizai Shimbun* published Tanaka's autobiography. All three papers were complimentary when Tanaka became prime minister in 1972 and were slow to publicize *Bungei Shunjū*'s revelations in mid 1974 of scandals involving Tanaka. Tanaka also reportedly "sold on" at later dates to such established institutions as Mitsui Bussan, Sanwa Bank, and the Palace Hotel (frequent meeting place of *zaikai* leaders). He did so by helping these organizations acquire prestigious sites for headquarters buildings on land close to the Imperial Palace which was formerly owned by the national government.

(2) Creation of the *Kankyō Eisei Kinyū Kōkō* (Environmental Sanitation Industry Financial Institution). One evening in 1968 Tanaka, as secretary general of the LDP, met with representatives of the all-Japan *ryokan*, teahouse, and bathhouse industry associations, who wanted assured access to low-cost government credit. In a single night's discussion, Tanaka hammered out an agreement with these groups to establish a special government financial institution to service their needs, which he later convinced the MOF to support. All the above pressure groups vigorously supported the Tanaka faction in the subsequent 1969 general election.

(3) The Bank of Japan special loan to Yamaichi Securities (1965). Only once in postwar history has the Bank of Japan granted a direct loan to a business firm other than a bank. The exception was made in 1965 at the express order of MOF minister Tanaka Kakuei. Yamaichi Securities, one of the "big four" securities firms, was threatened with collapse, because of the precipitous decline in Tokyo stock prices and transaction volume during

the early 1960s. Yamaichi and many private-sector financial leaders, such as Nakayama Sōhei, chairman of the Industrial Bank of Japan, wanted dramatic action to prevent financial panic. Tanaka provided it. He reportedly convinced the MOF and Bank of Japan bureaucrats to extend the unprecedented special loan to Yamaichi at a dramatic all-night meeting at MOF headquarters in Kasumigaseki.

(4) Tanaka brokerage during the U.S.-Japan textile crisis (1971). After less than six months as MITI minister, Tanaka was able in October 1971 to negotiate an agreement to restrain Japanese man-made fiber exports to the United States which both the American and the Japanese textile industries would accept. Ōhira Masayoshi and Miyazawa Kiichi, the MITI ministers preceding Tanaka, had been trying unsuccessfully to do this for nearly two years. Skillful use of the carrot (promise of large-scale government subsidies for the textile industry) and the stick (invocation of fears of strong U.S. sanctions against Japanese exports) secured domestic consensus on an agreement the Americans could accept. (For full details, see Destler, Fukui, and Satō 1979).

(5) Tanaka's road-tax proposal. In 1969 LDP Secretary General Tanaka proposed in the Diet introduction of a special road tax of ¥50,000 per motor vehicle per year. The Japan Auto Manufacturers' Association (JAMA) came out strongly in opposition and is reported to have sharply increased its contributions to the LDP's funding arm, the *Kokumin Kyōkai*, during 1970-1972. Tanaka proposed subsequently to reduce the auto tax to ¥15,000/year, and then let even that bill die quietly in the Diet, thus vindicating JAMA's foresight in cultivating Tanaka. By creating a crisis and then allowing it to die, Tanaka increased his financial support from business and, to some extent, his political support from business groups. (For details, see Tachibana 1976a:20.)

(6) Dealings with Lockheed (1972). In early 1972, Lockheed Aircraft's major commercial goals in Japan were: a) to sell its Tristar jet to All Nippon Airways (ANA), in competition with Douglas Aircraft's DC-10; and b) to sell its PXL anti-submarine-warfare (ASW) aircraft to the Japanese Defense Agency. Lockheed is reported to have approached Tanaka, through a major trading company, and offered him ¥500 million ($2.5 million) in return for his brokerage services. Tanaka appears to have been instrumental in convincing ANA to opt for the Tristar over the DC-10. ANA wanted new, high-traffic domestic routes, as well as the chance to fly overseas. These "resources" were being allocated by key Tanaka-faction Dietman Hashimoto Tomisaburō, the transport minister.

In the case of the PXL, Tanaka used foreign pressure (*gaiatsu*) to buttress his brokerage. The Defense Agency had reputedly decided tentatively against Lockheed's PXL, in favor of a domestically produced ASW aircraft. Tanaka, intervening, used Richard Nixon's growing impatience with the U.S.-Japan

> trade balance to sway the Defense Agency. At the Hawaii
> Summit on September 1, 1972, Tanaka and Nixon agreed that
> Japan should undertake a $320 million emergency aircraft
> import program, which Tanaka agreed would include the
> Lockheed PXL.

A striking trait of Tanaka's brokerage—one which promoted his rise to the prime ministership—has been his ability to *create* resources for allocation. Tanaka was the first MOF minister to aggressively use *koku yūchi* (national land) sales to advance his political position. His power to choose locations for public works projects made information concerning such projects a valued political resource Tanaka could allocate. Other resources created by Tanaka to be allocated by him included foreign-aid projects, emergency import programs, and administrative spots in government corporations. His "plan for remodeling the Japanese archipelago," announced in the early 1970s, massively expanded the range of resources that he and his associates could allocate.

Tanaka Kakuei and Fukuda Takeo are not the only significant conservative political brokers in recent Japanese history. Some brokers remained largely behind the scenes, like Nezu Kaiichirō, Gotō Keita, and Kobayashi Ataru, who rose during the depression on the strength of entrepreneurial ability at reorganizing bankrupt companies, and others like Kodama Yoshio, who were spawned by the fortunes of war.

Other brokers have played both private and public roles. Men like Kishi Nobusuke (industrial-policy and foreign-aid brokerage), Kawashima Shōjirō (real estate and foreign aid), Nakasone Yasuhiro (transportation), Mizuta Mikio (finance and broadcasting), Ikeda Hayato (finance), Satō Eisaku (transportation), Kōno Ichirō, Ono Bamboku, and others have been Diet leaders while at the same time being powerful in informal, private transactions.

Behind-the-scenes brokers (*kuromaku*) and brokers with a public role share two key traits: (1) an independent power base, usually financial (giving them initial resources to facilitate brokerage), and (2) institutionalized connections with key parts of the existing power structure (allowing them to influence that structure when necessary). The greater their financial backing and the stronger their bureaucratic connections, the more influential brokers have been in national decision making. Ex-bureaucrats have an advantage as brokers. Not surprisingly, the prime ministers who have exerted the greatest impact on post-Occupation policy formation (Yoshida, Kishi, Ikeda, Satō, and Fukuda) have been former bureaucrats. The only striking exception is Tanaka Kakuei.

Resource brokerage, like most of Japanese "compensation politics," has thus far been the province largely of Liberal Democratic Party politicians, mainly from rural constituencies, and behind-the-scenes conservative kingmakers.

Opposition politicians desiring material benefits from the government for their constituents, therefore, must work closely with the ruling conservatives behind the scenes. Sometimes they even join the conservatives formally, as Prime Minister Suzuki Zenkō did in December 1948.

With the waning of conservative power during the late 1960s and early 1970s, groups other than the ruling conservatives began participating significantly in brokerage, first at the local and subsequently at the national level. The growing significance of opposition groups in policy making may have been arrested by the conservative resurgence that began with the 1979 local elections and has continued through the LDP "double election" victory of June 1980. But in the consensus-oriented Japanese political system, which tends to respect established human relationships, opposition politicians during the early 1980s must still be consulted in a manner disproportionate to their declining legislative strength. The Japanese resource-brokerage process is also rendered more complex by the shift of the ruling LDP from a rural to an urban electoral base, a long-term trend quite clearly confirmed in the 1980 returns. This development presages both the rise of new types of conservative political brokers and a new range of demands on such brokers, perhaps with a considerably stronger consumer orientation than heretofore.

Conservative Political Brokerage
and the Evolution of the Japanese Economy

As was noted earlier, political brokers capable of interceding with the bureaucracy on behalf of private-sector interest groups have come to the fore in Japanese politics and persisted at the top in a remarkably consistent pattern. During 1952-1980, six politicians with particularly strong brokerage capabilities (Yoshida, Kishi, Ikeda, Satō, Tanaka, and Fukuda) held the prime ministership for a total of 22.5 years, for an average term of 3.75 years. The other four (Hatoyama, Ishibashi, Miki, and Ōhira), who were less active as brokers, held power for a total of 5.5 years, an average term of 1.375 years.

One criterion for judging the brokerage capabilities of Japanese politicians must be the quality of their ties with powerful ministries. Close, institutionalized ties to officials with regulatory clout and allocative power are a vital precondition to delivering the resources which private-sector interest groups desire. Each of the six "strong brokers" listed above had such ties. Yoshida was a former Foreign Ministry official, rising to the premiership during the Occupation era when that ministry controlled the avenues of approach to the all-powerful Allied Forces. Kishi was a former vice minister of the *Shōkō Shō* (Ministry of Commerce) who entered politics just when the *Shōkō Shō*'s postwar successor (MITI) was at the height of its control powers. Ikeda Hayato was an MOF alumnus during the same period, while Satō Eisaku hailed from the prewar Railway Ministry and the postwar Transport Ministry as the pattern of transport regulation was undergoing considerable flux. The strong personal networks binding Fukuda and Tanaka to strategic ministries have already been noted.

The five strong brokers hailing from the bureaucracy all served a full career in their respective ministries before entering politics. This gave them a chance to develop the tight web of bureaucratic ties necessary for effective brokerage, as well as to gain private-sector allies. Their ability to develop support networks was also aided by their elite university backgrounds; all were graduates of imperial universities, and all but Ikeda were from Tokyo University. Ōhira Masayoshi, by contrast, graduated from Hitotsubashi University and resigned early from MOF to enter politics. These two developments made it harder for him to create the personal networks so valuable for brokerage which the other five ex-bureaucrats possessed.

The reports of Japanese journalists and politicians also tend to confirm the unusual involvement in brokerage of the six strong brokers listed above. Ikeda, for example, was noted for his involvement in brokering government loans to industry during the credit-short, late 1940s, as were Fukuda and, at a later date, Kishi, Satō, and Tanaka. None of the prime ministers less active were so known. With the exception of Japan's 1956 recognition of the Soviet Union, engineered by Hatoyama, virtually all the major departures of postwar foreign and domestic policy have been made under "strong" brokers, suggesting once again their capabilities within the political system.

Of the leaders less active as brokers, all but Hatoyama were to a large extent temperamentally disinclined to play an active brokerage role. Ishibashi, a former journalist, disdained compensation-oriented aspects of the political process and may have been the most ideological of Japanese premiers; Miki, his *kobun* or younger confidante, was strikingly similar in orientation. Ōhira, also highly intellectual, was disposed to leave many aspects of brokerage to his political ally, Tanaka, and to leave issues to play themselves out in the political arena rather than actively brokering them. Hatoyama, although skilled at mediation, was handicapped by his own purge at the hands of the Occupation, the disruptive effect of the purge on his network of personal associates, and his relatively weak ties to strategic, economic, policy-making bodies like the Ministry of Finance.

Forces deep within Japanese society have been responsible for this striking prominence of brokers in the nation's political leadership. Strong cultural predispositions toward decision making outside the public view and against direct, confrontational resolution of conflict produce a great need for mediators of various types. Rapid economic growth has created new resources (expanded state budgets, newly valuable government land, and so on) for allocation, while at the same time creating gaps between regulatory policy and new economic realities crying out for brokerage. Bureaucratic power, coupled with unevenness in its application, has also intensified private–sector demand for resource brokers and helped those skilled at such mediation to move to the center of the political process.

This prominence of brokers in Japanese political processes has had several important consequences for the political economy:

(1) It has generally complicated the task of bureaucratic control, since brokers are tempted to arbitrate controls for the sake of political or material gain. This has, for example, clearly been true in the field of credit allocation where actions such as Tanaka's support for expansion of government small–business–oriented credit facilities has often undercut bureaucratic efforts to reshape industrial structures.

(2) It has often facilitated the operation of market mechanisms, albeit in somewhat politicized forms. For example, it has aided in the development of new entrepreneurial groups (the Fuyō Group, the Sanwa Group, and so on), rising in response to the operation of competitive forces, regularly allying themselves with brokers for protection against efforts by more established enterprises to suppress them.

(3) It tends to impart an expansionary, and often an inflationary, bias to Japanese economic policy because it creates a class of intermediaries whose tasks are facilitated by an expanding resource pie and vastly complicated if they are forced to mediate conflict–ridden, zero–sum allocation processes. This broker–induced bias toward expansion was clearest in 1971–1974, when Tanaka Kakuei was first MITI minister and then prime minister. Large–scale satisfaction of interest–group demands drove national budgets up 20–25 percent annually and induced a trend toward double–digit inflation well before the 1973 oil shock. But the bias surfaced at times even during the regimes of fiscal conservatives like Fukuda Takeo. This occurred, for example, in 1978, ironically just as the nation was entering an era of low growth and budgetary constraint. As competition for the LDP presidency with an expansionist Ōhira Masayoshi (backed by Tanaka) intensified and as foreign pressure for reflation also grew, Fukuda expanded public works expenditures massively and drew up a national budget projecting spending over 35 percent greater than revenue.
The expansionary bias of Japanese public policy induced by the prominence of brokers also induces a greater measure of order and harmony into Japan's domestic politics and its international economic relations than would otherwise be the case. Tanaka's expanding budgets, for example, had room for the welfare spending and aid to local governments which opposition parties wanted. Those budgets also provided for the foreign aid and the support for emergency imports into Japan

which foreign countries desired. The generous use of subsidies, facilitated by headlong fiscal expansion, also made domestic interest groups, such as the textile industry, tractible in their disputes with foreign countries.

There are important variations among Japanese conservative political brokers in their paths to political power and their leadership styles once in positions of responsibility. Broadly, Japanese conservative leadership divides between bureaucrats (*kanryō*), epitomized by Fukuda Takeo, and political entrepreneurs without elite backgrounds (*shomin*), epitomized by Tanaka Kakuei. *Kanryō* tend to rise predictably from outstanding academic backgrounds at Tokyo University to top-level posts in strategic ministries like MOF, and hence into politics. They tend to be technically proficient, often issues-oriented, and relatively passive in leadership style. *Shomin*, by contrast, are of necessity pragmatic, aggressive promoters, reliant for success on their ability to curry favor with an establishment to whom they are essentially outsiders. *Shomin* are of necessity more concerned with the dynamics of political power than with the substance of public issues and are, as a result, often more reliant on the bureaucracy in the formulation of concrete policy proposals than the former bureaucrats themselves.

The distinction between *kanryō* and *shomin* is also often important in analyzing the impact of conservative leadership on the Japanese political economy. Broadly, *shomin* tend to be more consistently expansionist because of their need to create resources to reinforce their essentially vulnerable political positions. *Kanryō*, because of their established status, can generally afford to be more dispassionate in their judgment of macroeconomic questions and occasionally oppose growth-oriented policies which they feel are leading the nation toward economic or political instability.

When the established status of individual *kanryō* in the political hierarchy is for some reason called into question, or when growth coincides strongly with the interests of the ministries they represent, such ex-bureaucrats often adopt the expansion-oriented policies more typical of *shomin*. Thus, Ikeda Hayato and Ōhira Masayoshi, two of the rare MOF alumni not part of the elite, Tokyo University alumni network, both led somewhat precarious political lives and tended to bolster their positions with elite business and bureaucratic groups through expansion-oriented policies. The orientation of Satō Eisaku and Kishi Nobusuke may also have been influenced by the expansionary bias of the Transportation and MITI Ministries from which they hailed. But while these *kanryō* may at times have pursued expansionary policies, they tended not to be as aggressively entrepreneurial in using such policies to build political IOUs as *shomin* like Tanaka.

A major dilemma for Japan in the 1980s is that the dominant pattern of high-growth-oriented political brokerage adopted by both *shomin* and, to a lesser degree, *kanryō* retains its political attractiveness even as it becomes increasingly inappropriate to the times. In an era of low economic growth rates, budgetary revenues are unlikely to be sufficient to resolve conflicts just by lavishly compensating the protagonists. And increasing claims on resources from new quarters, such as defense, may further reduce the funds available for politically attractive allocation. Yet Tanaka Kakuei, with the largest faction in the Diet (101 seats in both Houses combined in mid 1981) and informal political power undiminished by his legal travails, remains committed to the techniques which have brought him to the center of the Japanese political scene.

But Japan cannot avoid the dilemma by opting for Fukuda and his leadership style. Elite-status brokers can no longer, in an increasingly egalitarian and pluralistic society, command automatic respect because of their educational or bureaucratic credentials. Gradual deregulation of the economy since the early 1960s has also undermined *kanryō* capabilities. In addition, the passing of the closely knit "purge-survivor" generation, now in its seventies, is disrupting closely knit networks of business contacts that ex-bureaucrats have long mobilized to enhance their influence.

Substantial political entrepreneurship of a variety alien to the experience of both *kanryō* and *shomin* of the past generation will most likely be required as the 1980s progress. Politicians will have to focus the concerns of the electorate increasingly on matters other than material compensation so as to moderate the political implications of the extremely slow growth of the resource pie. At times leaders may need to induce the electorate to accept sacrifice. Nakagawa Ichirō, as Agriculture Minister presiding over reduction in the real rice price during the late 1970s, and Watanabe Michio, as Finance Minister laying groundwork for tax increases in the early 1980s, provide examples of the sort of flamboyant, relatively charismatic "brokers of the scarcity era" who could emerge, and of their leadership style.

Like conservative brokers of the recent past, emerging brokers of the future such as Watanabe and Nakagawa maintain close ties with the bureaucracy. But they appeal to bureaucrats not so much because of the direct compensation they provide as for their ability to assure passage of politically unpalatable legislation desired by bureaucrats. The brokers obtain support for this through appeals to nationalism, aspirations for a more just society, and other nonacquisitive sentiments, as well as through more traditional compensation-oriented brokerage.

The evolution of Japanese conservative politics away from a preoccupation with material compensation should be aided by the gradual transformation of the ruling LDP into an urban-based party. Many new supporters of the party are relatively young blue- and white-collar urban workers, many in service industries, who are not organized to demand benefits from government. This transformation also reduces the relative influence of highly organized rural constituencies which have consistently pressured the conservative regime for large agricultural subsidies.

The dynamics of Japanese conservative leadership in the 1980s could well differ significantly from those of the previous generation, if only because of the new strategic problems relating to low growth which that leadership now confronts. But cultural predispositions toward indirect, nonconfrontationist decision making, together with structural peculiarities of the Japanese economy, will assure the continued prominence of political brokers. And as long as Japan has a clear conservative establishment with "insiders" and "outsiders" vying for political status, many essentials of the *kanryō* vs. *shomin* struggle for primacy will continue to reappear long after Fukuda Takeo and Tanaka Kakuei have passed from the political scene.

References

Destler, I. M., Haruhiro Fukui, and Hideo Satō. 1979. *The textile wrangle.* Ithaca: Cornell University Press.

Destler, I. M., Hideo Satō, Priscilla Clapp, and Haruhiro Fukui. 1976. *Managing an alliance.* Washington, D.C.: The Brookings Institution.

Fukui Haruhiro. 1970. *Party in power: The Japanese liberal democrats and policy-making.* Berkeley: University of California Press.

Gendai Seiji Kenkyū Kai, ed. 1976. *Tanaka Kakuei: sono eikō to zasetsu* (The glory and disgrace of Tanaka Kakuei). Tokyo: Kokusai Shōgyō Shuppan.

Hatakeyama Takeshi. 1975. *Habatsu no uchimaku* (The inside story of factions). Tokyo: Tachikaze Shobō.

Hyōron Shinsa. 1973- . *Kokkai giin sōran* (Diet members almanac). Tokyo: Nihon Minsei Kenkyū Kai.

Ikuzō Tajiri. 1978. Daifuku no kenkyū (Research on Ōhira and Fukuda). *Bungei Shunjū,* September.

Katō Yoshiyuki. 1973. *Tanaka Kakuei.* Tokyo: Sankō Sha.

Lowi, Theodore. 1972. Four systems of policy, politics, and choice. *Public Administration Review,* 32 (July-August).

Mainichi Shimbun Sha Seiji Bu. 1975. *Seihen* (A political incident). Tokyo: Mainichi Shimbun Sha.

Mayumi Yoshihiko. 1972. *Ningen Tanaka Kakuei* (The human side of Tanaka Kakuei). Tokyo: Diamondo Sha.

Miyasaka Masayuki. 1970. *Seifu-Jimintō-zaikai* (Government-LDP-business world). Tokyo: Sanichi Shobō.

Najita Tetsuo. 1967. *Hara Kei in the politics of compromise.* Cambridge, Massachusetts: Harvard University Press.

Nihon Ginkō Tōkei Kyoku. 1979. *Keizai tōkei nenpō* (Economic statistics annual). Tokyo: Nihon Ginkō Tōkei Kyoku.

Ninagawa Masao. 1976. *Tanaka Kakuei shinazu* (Tanaka Kakuei doesn't die). Tokyo: Yamate Shobō.

Ochi Michio. 1973. *Chichi: Fukuda Takeo* (Father: Fukuda Takeo). Tokyo: Sankei Shimbun Sha.

Ōkurashō Shukei Kyoku. 1979. *Zaisei tōkei* (Financial statistics). Tokyo: Ōkurashō.

Pempel, T. J., ed. 1977. *Policymaking in contemporary Japan.* Ithaca: Cornell University Press.

Roberts, John G. 1973. *Mitsui.* New York: Weatherhill.

Satō Yūichi. 1976. *Fukuda Takeo ron* (An explanation of Fukuda Takeo). Tokyo: Jutaku Shinpo Sha.

Seirōkyō Chōsa Honbu. 1979. *Chōsa jihō* (Current Research). Tokyo: Seifu Kankei Tokushu Hōjin Rōdō Kumiai Kyōgi Kai.

Tachibana Takashi. 1976a. *Tanaka Kakuei kenkyū* (Research on Tanaka Kakuei), Vols. I and II. Tokyo: Kōdansha.

_____. 1976b. Shin Tanaka Kakuei kenkyū (New research on Tanaka Kakuei). *Bungei Shunjū*, September, 114–35.

Tahara Sōichirō. 1978. *Kool na saishō kōhō* (The cool candidate for the top job). Tokyo: Gakuyō Shobō.

Tanaka Hiroshi, ed. 1974. *Hoshu kakumei ni kakeru* (Betting on conservative revolution). Tokyo: Yomiuri Shimbun Sha.

_____. 1977. *Fukuda Takeo: hoshu saisei ni tatsu* (Fukuda Takeo: standing at the rebirth of Japanese conservatism). Tokyo: Yomiuri Shimbun Sha.

Tanaka Kakuei. 1966. *Watashi no rirekisho* (My autobiography). Tokyo: Nihon Keizai Shimbun Sha.

_____. 1972. *Rettō kaizō ron* (A plan for remodeling the Japanese archipelago). Tokyo: Nikkan Kōgyō Shimbun Sha.

Thayer, Nathaniel B. 1969. *How the conservatives rule Japan.* Princeton, New Jersey: Princeton University Press.

Togawa Isatake. 1972a. *Sōri Tanaka Kakuei* (Prime Minister Tanaka Kakuei). Tokyo: Kōdansha.

_____. 1972b. *Tanaka Kakuei den* (The story of Tanaka Kakuei). Tokyo: Tsuru Shobō.

_____. 1973. *Tanaka Kakuei: Mogoku* (The violent pronouncements of Tanaka Kakuei). Tokyo: Shobunsha.

Urate Susumi. 1978. *Fukuda Takeo.* Tokyo: Kokusai Shōgyō Shuppan.

APPENDIX A:
THE RISE OF FUKUDA TAKEO AND TANAKA KAKUEI
TO LEADERSHIP STATUS (to 1955)

Year	Events in Fukuda's Career	Events in Tanaka's Career
1904	Born in Gunma Prefecture.	
1918	Attending middle school in Takasaki, Gunma Prefecture.	Born in Niigata Prefecture.
1926	Graduates from Ikkō (First Imperial High School), Tokyo.	Enters elementary school in rural Niigata Prefecture.
1929	Graduates from Tokyo University Faculty of Law, first in his class.	Attending rural elementary school.
1930	Financial attache, Japanese Embassy, London.	
1933	Returns from London to become director, Kyoto Tax Office. Marries Arai Mitsue, daughter of a judge in Gumma Prefecture.	Working as day laborer in construction, after graduating from middle school at fifteen (5/33). Subsequently works for the magazine *Hi no De* (Rising Sun).
1934	Becomes head of the Yokohama Tax Office.	Goes to Tokyo to civil-engineering school and to seek his fortune. (In 1954 Tanaka becomes honorary principal of this school.)
1938	Budget examiner for Army Ministry.	Passes officer's physical for naval commission, but gives up enlistment plans because of mother's illness.
1939		Drafted into Imperial Army and sent to Manchuria.
1941	Sent to China as advisor on financial policy to the Japanese-supported Nanking government.	Given army medical discharge after near-fatal bout with pneumonia. Returns to menial job in construction.
1942		Marries Sakamoto Hana, daughter of prosperous contractor.

APPENDIX A (continued)

Year	Events in Fukuda's Career	Events in Tanaka's Career
1943	Becomes section chief within MOF Ministerial Secretariat.	Establishes Tanaka Doken Kōgyō (Tanaka Civil Construction).
1944	Becomes secretary to the Minister of Finance.	Awarded ¥22 million contract to relocate piston-ring plant from Japan to Taejon, Korea.
1945	Bureau chief, MOF Secretariat.	Returns to Japan as expatriate from Korea, reputedly having retained a large advance tendered before war's end for relocation of the Taejon piston-ring plant.
1946	Becomes Banking Bureau chief.	Loses in initial try for Diet seat, as Progressive Party (*Shimpo Tō*) candidate.
1947	Chosen bureau chief, MOF Budget Bureau. Strongly favored candidate for MOF administrative vice minister, the most prestigious position in the Japanese bureaucracy.	Elected to the Diet. At twenty-eight the youngest member of the body.
1948		Implicated in the Tankō Kokkan (Coal Mining Administration) incident. Resigns as parliamentary vice minister, Ministry of Justice, to accept responsibility.
1950	Arrested in the Shōwa Denkō scandal. Resigns from MOF without becoming administrative vice minister.	Becomes president of Nagaoka Railways.
1951		Introduces three member bills dealing with construction and housing.
1952	Elected to Diet for first time, from Gumma Prefecture.	
1953	Joins Liberal Party, after being elected twice as an independent.	

APPENDIX A (continued)

Year	Events in Fakuda's Career	Events in Tanaka's Career
1954	Founding member of the Japan Democratic Party, together with Kishi Nobusuke, Ashida Hitoshi, and Ishibashi Tanzan.	

Sources: Mayumi 1972:218-30; and Satō 1976:230-34.

APPENDIX B:
CAREER PROGRESSION OF FUKUDA TAKEO AND TANAKA KAKUEI
WITHIN THE LDP, 1955-80

Year	Fukuda Career Path	Tanaka Career Path
1955		5/55 - Becomes chairman, House of Representatives Committee on Commerce and Industry.
1956	Vice chairman, Policy Affairs Research Council (Ishibashi Cabinet).	
1957	2/57 - Deputy secretary general, LDP.	7/57-7/60 - Post and Tele-communications minister, Kishi Cabinet. One month after becoming minister, sings naniwa bushi (country music) on NHK radio.
1958	6/58 - Chairman, PARC (Kishi Cabinet).	
1959	1/59 - Secretary general, LDP.	
1960	12/60-7/61 - Chairman, PARC (Ikeda Cabinet). Resigns in opposition to high-growth policy.	
1962		7/62-8/65 - MOF minister in Ikeda Cabinet, charged with helping put income doubling plan into effect. Also chair-man of special Diet com-mittee on Water and Natural Resources.
1965	6/65-8/66 - MOF minister (Satō Cabinet).	8/65 - Named secretary general, LDP.
1966	12/66 - Appointed secretary general, LDP (replacing Tanaka Kakuei).	12/66 - Resigns as LDP secretary general in connec-tion with the "black mist" scandal.

APPENDIX B (continued)

Year	Fukuda Career Path	Tanaka Career Path
1967		9/67 - Appointed head of the LDP's Urban Policy Research Committee and of its study committee on the Tokyo metropolitan area.
1968	11/68-7/71 - MOF minister.	11/68 - Becomes chairman, LDP Rice Price Committee, and secretary general, LDP (holding latter position until 7/71).
1971	7/71-7/72 - Foreign minister, during Nixon shocks and conclusion of textile crisis.	7/71-7/72 - MITI minister (Third Satō Cabinet).
1972	7/72 - Defeated, at sixty-seven, in LDP presidential election by Tanaka Kakuei.	7/72 - Victorious in LDP presidential election. At fifty-four, youngest prime minister in modern Japanese history.
1973	11/73-7/74 - MOF minister (Tanaka Cabinet).	
1974	12/74-10/76 - Deputy prime minister and EPA chief (Miki Cabinet).	8/74 - Injured politically by *Bungei Shunjū* revelations on personal finances; 11/74 - resigns as prime minister.
1976	12/76-12/78 - Prime minister.	8/76 - Arrested in connection with Lockheed scandal.
1978	10/78 - Defeated in primary election for LDP president by Ōhira Masayoshi, who was backed strongly by Tanaka Kakuei.	10/78 - Engineers defeat of Fukuda Takeo in LDP presidential primary.
1979	10/79 - Unsuccessfully demands Ōhira's resignation, in wake of election returns disappointing to LDP.	

APPENDIX B (continued)

Year	Fukuda Career Path	Tanaka Career Path
1980	5/80 - Abstains, together with his faction and Miki faction, on Diet vote of no confidence in Ōhira, helping precipitate general election. 7/80 - Supports establishment of Suzuki Zenkō regime, following Ōhira's death. Advent of this regime moderates Fukuda's breach with Tanaka and former Ōhira factions.	7/80 - Supports establishment of Suzuki Zenkō government.

Comments

(1) Fukuda's major responsibility within the LDP has been to define issues rather than to maneuver politically. His party posts have centered on policy definition.

(2) Fukuda's Cabinet responsibilities have been concentrated in the financial field. Fukuda has four and one-half years experience as MOF minister and is the foremost expert in the LDP on finance.

(3) Macro-economic policy orientation: no vested interest in headlong growth. Early in his career Fukuda manifested his misgivings in this area by resigning as the Ikeda Cabinet's PARC chairman, July 1961.

(1) Tanaka's party responsibilities have been primarily organizational. Served three times as LDP secretary general, for a total of over four years.

(2) Tanaka has held wide range of Cabinet posts, not concentrated in any one policy area; three years as MOF minister and one year as MITI minister (during Nixon shocks and textile crisis) were crucial to his rise. Never served as foreign minister.

(3) Macro-economic policy orientation: strongly growth oriented. Tanaka has long record of supporting aggressive monetary and fiscal expansion, even at the cost of substantial inflation.

Sources: Mayumi 1972:218-30; and Satō 1976:203-34.

LIBERAL DEMOCRATS IN DISARRAY:
INTERGENERATIONAL CONFLICT IN THE CONSERVATIVE CAMP

Susan J. Pharr

The path is treacherous, but being fully aware of its
dangers we want to move steadily forward, step by step.
Kōno Yōhei, August 1976

On June 14, 1976, six members of the Liberal Democratic Party (LDP), the
conservative party in power, held a press conference and announced their
intention to leave the party. A week later the six, with the press in tow, appeared
at LDP headquarters in Tokyo and formally resigned from the party. Three days
later, on June 25, they announced the formation of a new conservative political
group, the New Liberal Club (NLC). With the next general election for the lower
house of Japan's bicameral Diet only five months away, they began a frantic
effort to draw other conservatives to their cause. The NLC managed to find
twenty-five candidates willing to throw their lot in with the rebels.[1] In the lower-
house election on December 5, 1976, seventeen of them were elected—a showing
that was below the twenty seats necessary to secure full legislative status for the
NLC within the Diet, but one widely hailed by the media as a stunning victory for

The fieldwork for this paper was undertaken in Japan in the spring and summer of
1978 with a grant from the Japan Foundation. A grant from the Graduate School
of the University of Wisconsin-Madison supported the analysis of interview data
and published source materials in the summers of 1979 and 1980. I would like to
thank Richard Meher, Satō Ikuko, Oyadomari Motoko, and Kishima Takako for
their able research assistance at various stages of the project. My work on status
politics in Japan has been greatly aided by the comments and suggestions of
Richard Merelman, Murray Edelman, Ellis Krauss, T.J. Pempel, Hans Baerwald,
Patricia Steinhoff, Ishida Takeshi, and Uchida Mitsuru.
1. To have the right to put forward candidates in an election, a political group
must offer a minimum of twenty-five candidates in a lower-house election, or ten
candidates in an upper-house election (Wagatsuma 1967:94).

the Club and yet another blow to the beleaguered LDP.[2] Indeed, only through a postelection roundup of conservative independents was the Liberal Democratic Party able to hold its majority in the lower house.[3]

Despite the attention that the NLC commanded at the time of its debut and the massive media coverage in Japan that followed its efforts to secure a foothold in the political landscape, those efforts have met only limited success. By early 1979, the media assessment was harsh. Summing up the view of many critics, the *Yomiuri* observed that the Club lacked the indispensible three "S's"— *seisaku* (policy), *soshiki* (organizational structure), and *shikin* (funds)—to make it as a party in Japan (*Yomiuri Shimbun*, March 8, 1979). In the lower-house election in October 1979, the NLC captured only four seats. The party's leader, Kōno Yōhei, resigned the post in November to take responsibility for the defeat and to meditate on the group's future (*Asahi Shimbun*, November 27, 1979). Demoralized by its loss of momentum after such a promising beginning and plagued by internal problems, the NLC for a time appeared near the end of its short life. Although it partially recouped its losses by gaining twelve seats in the June 1980 lower-house election, its ultimate fate is still uncertain.

The NLC has rarely been a significant actor or broker in Japanese politics,[4] and its electoral hold has been miniscule. As a symptom of fundamental tensions in Japanese society and politics, however, the conflict that led to the emergence of the New Liberal Club invites close study. The NLC breakaway may be seen as a stage in a multidimensional political conflict. At one level, it was only one of numerous creaks and strains affecting the giant LDP, with its many warring factions. Since the party's base of support had been steadily eroding over the period prior to the breakaway, internal conflicts could have been expected to intensify in disputes over who was to be held accountable for the decline and over how further losses were to be arrested. At another level, the breakaway was a power play—the effort of a small group of mavericks to jockey for a more powerful position in the conservative camp. At a deeper level, however, the break may be seen as a manifestation of intergenerational conflict within the LDP (and in Japanese organizations more generally) over the nature of leadership in Japan: over who leads, the style and terms of leadership, mobility into leadership ranks

2. To have the right to introduce legislation, a political group must hold at least twenty seats in the lower house and ten in the upper house (Wagatsuma 1967:94).
3. The LDP won 249 seats in the election, 7 seats short of a majority. When twelve independents joined the party following the election, the party's total increased to 261 seats, giving the LDP a 5-seat majority in the lower house.
4. The possible exception to this general conclusion was the role played by the NLC in the election of Ōhira as prime minister in 1979, in which the NLC's vote for Ōhira contributed to his win over Fukuda.

and the pace at which it is to be achieved, and the expectations surrounding followership. The intergenerational aspect of the conflict is the focus here.

Although other factors contributed to the decision of the original six LDP members to leave the party, the break and the stages leading up to it can be seen as an episode in "status politics" in which a central issue was the distribution and prerogatives of authority based on age and rank (Pharr, forthcoming). Kōno Yōhei, his two chief lieutenants, and most of the politicians subsequently drawn to the NLC were men in their thirties and forties. The original departure from the LDP culminated a conflict involving numerous grievances associated with their status as juniors in an age-graded party hierarchy. The episode was one manifestation of general conflict in Japanese organizational life between "Young Turks," on the one hand, and senior Japanese political and economic leaders, on the other.

Analyzing the steps leading to the breakaway of the NLC from the Liberal Democratic Party is a way of studying how leadership is exercised and what tensions between leaders and followers may be manifest in Japan today. The study is based on interviews conducted in 1978 with some thirty people (members of the NLC and the LDP; their secretaries; scholars; members of the press) involved in the conflict or close observers of it, and on published source materials.

Social and political conflicts unfold in well-understood contexts and stages (Coleman 1957; Kriesberg 1973; Coser 1967; DiPalma 1973). They begin when potentially conflicting parties develop incompatible goals in some situation. The latent conflict may or may not become manifest, and one principal task of analysis is specifying the conditions under which conflict does arise. In a second stage, the conflict becomes manifest, and the parties recognize that they have incompatible goals. In the third stage the parties initiate conflict behavior; among the pertinent characteristics of this stage are the methods (persuasion, coercion, reward) the parties adopt to pursue their goals, the degree to which the conflict is institutionalized, and the possible role of third parties.

In the fourth stage the conflict escalates and deescalates with changes in its intensity and scope, and in a fifth stage it terminates. Although one conflict may well begin a new one, any specific conflict has some kind of outcome. Finally, the effects of the conflict feed back into the objective conditions from which it arose, and potentially cause further conflicts. This feedback process, by which social structures and values undergo adjustments, provides the central dynamic of social change.

In the conflict that led to the breakaway of the New Liberal Club, the objective condition, or *first stage*, can be located in the age-based status relations within the Liberal Democratic Party and within Japanese organizations more generally. In the typical Japanese pattern the distribution of authority heavily favors senior leaders who monopolize the stakes of politics—money, power, and position—and allocate them, on the basis of position on an age-graded hierarchy, to their subordinates. Subordinates ideally are expected to acknowledge—indeed, celebrate—the authority of their superiors through various forms of deference, by which juniors demonstrate their loyalty and show obedience to their seniors. The senior generation in the LDP—men sixty and over, with many key figures in their seventies—mete out rewards to their juniors in the context of the much-researched factional arrangements of Japanese politics. The conflict latent in the inequality based on age and status became manifest in the NLC breakaway because some factors that today affect age juniors in the LDP had particular differential impact on the group who left it. These factors moved the conflict into the *second stage*. The *third stage*, initiating conflict behavior, unfolded during the five years or so prior to 1976 in which junior LDP members organized themselves and challenged the terms of status relations within the party. In the *fourth stage*, which may be dated from the fall of 1974, the conflict escalated as the group began a series of steps that led to their ultimate departure from the party. This escalation was in large part a response to media attention. In the *fifth stage* the conflict terminated when the six dissidents who left the LDP created a new conservative group. The aftermath of the conflict involved the movement of additional junior men and other malcontents out of the LDP and into the New Liberal Club and the continuing tension between the fledgling group and its parent party.

Stage One: The Objective Basis for Conflict

When young men are elected to the Diet on the LDP ticket for the first time, they enter a bewildering maze of activity and intrigue. In the number and percentage of Diet seats it controls, the conservative party is a giant compared to most parties in ruling coalitions in European multiparty systems. In 1966, when Kōno Yōhei was laying the groundwork for his first election to the Diet the following year, the LDP held 282 seats (out of 486) in the lower house. Newcomers enter a veritable ocean of fellow LDP members, most hoping to secure positions of power and influence within the ruling party. The LDP has been in power continuously from 1955, and with assured majorities, its reward structure has been rather clearcut. The prime ministership, all cabinet positions, legislative posts, party posts, and control over policy directions for Japan itself all have been within the power domain of the LDP. To those newly elected on the LDP ticket (and in stark contrast to what awaits those elected on other parties' tickets in Japan), the potential rewards are dazzling.

To allocate their leadership positions, most national legislatures employ some kind of seniority principle. Even those that do not formally rely on seniority consider experience to be a major prerequisite for high positions. In Japan, however, in accordance with organizational principles that operate throughout the society, what is unusual is the degree to which the seniority principle guides the allocation of party rewards, the amount of power concentrated in age superiors, and the extent to which access to leadership is limited by factors beyond the power of individuals to change—specifically, political age (number of times elected) and biological age.

The distribution of posts and other rewards is handled through the various factions into which the party has been divided at any given time, each headed by a senior LDP Diet member. Since the factions operate outside the formal party organization, the allocation process bypasses formal party rules, following informal rules developed and applied by status superiors that are not subject to challenge or modification by those below. Although the official position of the LDP is to deplore (and on occasions, to outlaw) factions, they remain the party's mechanism for distributing posts. Party, Diet, and governmental positions, including the prime ministership, are parcelled out among the faction heads on the basis of factional strength. The faction heads then distribute the faction's share of positions to the faction members waiting below.

Nathaniel Thayer has described the evolution of factions in the Liberal Democratic Party after its creation in 1955:

> As the formal structure began to emerge, it also became hierarchial; politicians standing at the peak of the hierarchy got first shot at the cabinet and favored party posts. Position in the hierarchy was ultimately determined by the faction leader. He gave consideration to age and to the number of times a Dietman had been elected, common standards that are used throughout the party. But more important criteria were length of time in the faction and degree of service to the faction. A new faction member started at the bottom of the pecking order. (Thayer 1969:23)

As Thayer notes, position in a faction's hierarchy is determined by considerations of political and biological age, and by performance criteria. Thayer emphasizes the importance of performance criteria, in the form of service to the faction. But it is more significant that although performance criteria provide a basis for making adjustments in rank, they almost never determine it. Figuratively speaking, each newly elected LDP member is assigned a number within his faction, and then waits in line until his number is called. He may be moved up in the queue because of his performance, but the queue itself is basic to the structure of authority within the LDP, and there is no way to avoid it entirely, no matter how exceptional the performance, nor how faithful the service.

The relation between the biological age and political age of Dietmen is complex. Normally in Japanese organizations, biological age and time in rank are congruent. At the top of the organizational pyramid are the oldest persons, who are also the persons with the most experience; at the bottom are those who, both in terms of biological age and time in grade, are the most junior. People of approximately the same age are hired into an organization with roughly equivalent levels of skill and move up the organizational ladder from a common base point. However, because of the nature of Diet membership, which is almost never a first career for anyone, biological age and time in rank are often out of sync, notably in the case of persons who enter the Diet in their late forties or early fifties after a long period in the bureaucracy, and thus who are senior biologically, but junior in terms of time-in-grade. This incongruence is resolved by giving priority to political age—specifically, the number of times elected to the Diet—and then differentiating among those in the same term on the basis of biological age (interview with LDP Diet member Ōtsubo Kenichirō, June 4, 1978).

The distribution of power in such a system is fairly clear-cut. Top leadership positions are in the hands of those members who are senior in political age and normally in biological age. Seniority does not insure leadership positions and influence, but it is an essential precondition for them. At the very top of the power structure are a small group of senior men who function as power brokers in the most hotly contested leadership struggle of all: the race among the faction heads to be prime minister. Some of the power brokers head factions themselves, but not all faction heads are included in this small circle. Ex-prime ministers figure prominently in it. At the next level are the faction heads taken collectively, who compete for key posts themselves and who allocate rewards to the rest of the LDP members below them in their respective factions. These two groups of seniors, about fifteen or fewer LDP Diet members normally both old and often reelected, wield the power to distribute rewards and to make critical decisions relating to the party. Moreover, since rewards are distributed to those below who have been waiting in line for the longest periods of time, most are allocated to men who are themselves senior, as those further below watch and wait.

The inequality inherent in the power arrangements of this type of age-graded hierarchy provides the structural basis for conflict on the part of status inferiors. Various forces, however, normally prevent conflicts from becoming open ones. First, traditional Japanese norms give legitimacy to this authority arrangement. Status differences based on age, sex, and other ascriptive criteria, which were part of the feudal order that prevailed prior to 1868, were carried forward into the modern period and were affirmed in official ideology and taught in Japanese schools until the end of World War II. The norms and values of prewar Japan reinforced the age-graded hierarchies that were ubiquitous in Japanese life, teaching status inferiors to accept their lot.

Second, junior Diet members normally can expect concrete rewards for participating in the arrangement. Juniors ideally are expected to acknowledge the authority exercised by their status superiors in a number of ritualized ways: by using deference terms, bowing more deeply than the superior, and displaying an attitude of alertness and readiness to commands and wishes, expressed and unexpressed, of superiors. The behavioral expectation is that they subordinate their personal desires or preferences to those of the faction, as interpreted by its leader. The rewards of such obedience, however, are considerable. Money is distributed by faction heads to members to pay their campaign and other political expenses. Many young faction members in the Diet today say openly that this is the primary reason that they belong to a faction. It also secures them the LDP endorsement, which is seen as essential for mobilizing electoral support for conservative candidates. Moreover, faction membership permits juniors to participate in Diet politics. As Thayer, quoting veteran LDP member Matsuda Takechiyo, has noted, young Diet members "have no chance to speak, because debate has gone out of style in the Diet. They have no way of learning their trade . . . They have no forum for their ideas. They get no important assignments because they have no political experience. They have nothing to do. Nothing to do and no place to be. It's no wonder they drift to factions" (Thayer 1969:40–41). Seen in this light, factional membership may be a bad bargain, because it offers juniors only limited participation, but it is better than no bargain at all.

Belonging to a faction also satisfies the psychological need for belongingness. As several junior Diet members interviewed for this study asserted, the LDP's large number of representatives makes it impossible for the individual to relate to the group as a whole. Factions, however, provide a framework within which the individual can establish a place. The ultimate and essential reward factional membership promises, of course, is that leadership positions will eventually come, even to those at the back of the queue.

Since factional membership offers immediate financial, political, and psychological rewards and holds out greater benefits in the future, and since there is almost no other way to gain these benefits within the present order, then it is astonishing to find junior Diet members openly voicing objections to the terms of factional membership and calling for reform of the party's distribution of leadership. That a small group of junior members defied the LDP's status system, renouncing their future in it, demonstrates an unusual level of dissatisfaction, which demands explanation.

Stage Two: The Conflict Becomes Manifest

When the original six members of the New Liberal Club broke with the LDP in 1976, the media hailed them as challenging the party's gerontocracy. LDP leaders, said the respected journal *Ekonomisuto*, were a "group of grandfathers" whose views were no longer those of the nation (July 7, 1977:34). Younger LDP members, noted one writer, applauded the departure of Kōno Yōhei and his colleagues from the LDP, as did younger people in business circles and among the public. Surveys assessing the new group's following confirmed that the group had strong support among younger voters (Hosojima 1976:10-14; Hashimoto 1976:12-16).

This response to the breakaway suggests that the conflict inherent in junior-senior relations is widely perceived in today's Japan. The media readily interpreted the move as involving intergenerational conflict and a challenge to the structure of party authority, and the public, especially younger voters, understood the rationale for the break well enough to support Kōno and the other junior men who left. This awareness is the result of value changes that have occurred in postwar Japan. The norms that made hierarchical authority legitimate came under attack during the Allied Occupation (1945-1952). Democracy became the official ideology of the state, and the principle of egalitarianism, incorporated in the laws and transmitted by the schools, challenges the authority exercised by seniors in junior-senior relationships. People educated after World War II thus have an ideological basis for questioning the legitimacy of such authority, even if they are not prepared to challenge it directly in their own daily lives.

This value change has created an environment in which status-related grievances are familiar and initiatives by status inferiors to improve their lot attract the sympathy of many people, especially the young. That these grievances surfaced in the LDP has several causes: first, some structural changes occurred in the party that may have exacerbated its age-related tensions; second, changes in the reward structure made the status quo less attractive for young people; and finally, these changes adversely affected a small group of juniors who, unlike most of their peers, had little to lose from voicing their grievances.

Intergenerational conflict within the LDP emerged as an increasingly important issue as its leadership aged. The LDP was formed out of two conservative parties in 1955. Purges of conservatives following World War II and the general shake-up in Japan's leadership during the Occupation meant that the new party was initially dominated by men in their fifties, who made up 41.4 percent of the party's membership in 1956 (see Table 1). Less than 5 percent of the membership were seventy and over. The party's Diet membership has subsequently aged steadily. Many in their fifties in 1956 were still around in 1976, when almost 12 percent were men in their seventies. The LDP's growing gerontocracy has received attention in the media, undoubtedly heightening the perception of junior members that the party leadership is dominated, and its reward structure controlled, by a generation of grandfathers.

Changes in the party's age structure have been accompanied by changes affecting its reward system. Factions, as noted earlier, usually offer financial, political, and psychological rewards that in the past have offset the potential dissatisfactions of junior status. Maximum benefits from these rewards are realized when certain conditions are met. For example, factional funds are of greatest significance to a Diet member relying on them for campaign expenses. A junior with extensive independent financial resources or little forthcoming party resources will see fewer advantages in factional membership. Second, LDP endorsement and active campaign support are most rewarding if and when they are necessary for, or contribute to, electoral success. If they do not promote electoral success, or if the junior member can win without them, their political benefit is less compelling. Third, that factional membership permits meaningful participation in the political life of the Diet is a benefit inversely related to the number of alternative opportunities for participation. And finally, the future rewards of factional membership cannot be attractive unless junior members feel secure in the belief that the senior generations command and distribute them.

TABLE 1

Age Distribution within the LDP, 1956–1976

(in percent)

Generations	1956	1966	1976
Senior (60 & over)	28.6	39.0	40.6
Middle (50–59)	41.4	39.4	33.6
Junior (under 50)	30.0	21.6	25.8
	100.0	100.0	100.0

Source: Nihon Seikei Shimbun, *Kokkai Binran*, Tokyo: Nihon Seikei Shimbunsha, 1956, 1966, and 1978. (Data in the 1978 edition were ages as of December 5, 1976.)

These considerations help explain why juniors within the LDP at the time of the breakaway were finding declining satisfaction from factional arrangements, and thus felt fewer constraints about expressing grievances. Recent changes in the law had seriously undermined the ability of faction heads to provide financially for their members. The Political Funds Control Law passed during Miki Takeo's prime ministership forced disclosure of the names of contributors to the party and set limits on donations from individuals and companies. In 1976, the year of the breakaway, the factions reportedly raised only half the amount they had collected the previous year, and the fund raising of the LDP itself was at ¥7,800 million ($30.6 million), down 32 percent from the previous year (Davies 1977:21). The financial rewards of factional membership, then, were substantially reduced. Nor did the LDP endorsement appear so critical as the party's electoral base declined and bribery scandals diminished the value of having famous party members, often the faction head, stump on the behalf of the candidate. The attractions of factional membership had also declined. In the 1970s, largely as a response to the needs of younger members to have a forum for discussing policy, a number of study groups were formed in the Diet. Examples are the Hirakawa Society, established in 1973, which has ties to the Ōhira faction, Seirankai, with ties to the Fukuda faction, and the Shimpū (New Breeze) Political Study Association, with ties to the Tanaka faction. Although membership in these groups does not lead to party posts, it helps meet affiliational needs that were once satisfied wholly through the factions proper. Finally, as Kōno Yōhei has noted, the party's enjoinder to "Wait, wait" (*Matte, matte*) commands obedience only when a junior member of the Diet believes that waiting will pay off (interview with Kōno Yōhei, June 5, 1978). As the LDP's electoral margin declined in the period prior to the breakaway, seniors' ability to command and distribute party posts ten to twenty years in the future to those waiting below inevitably was open to question, leading young LDP Diet members to speculate about what other alternative routes to power might be open to them. Among these alternatives, forming or joining a new conservative party—once an unthinkable heresy—was no longer wholly outside the range of possibilities.

The changes described affected all junior LDP members. To determine why the Kōno Six, and not others, decided to abandon the party, it is necessary to look more particularly at the rebels.

The breakaway was led by Kōno Yōhei, who was thirty-nine in 1976, and his two chief lieutenants, Yamaguchi Toshio, then thirty-six, and Nishioka Takeo, age forty. Kōno and Yamaguchi were both in their third term of office, while Nishioka was in his fourth. In addition to their youth, the men shared certain characteristics ("Shin jiyū kurabu tettei kenkyū," *Bungei Shunjū* 1977:92-121). First and foremost, all three were *nisei*, that is, second-generation politicians, sons of famous political fathers. Kōno's father, Kōno Ichirō, was an especially famous LDP politician who, at the time of his death in 1965, headed one of the LDP's most powerful factions. The implications of being a *nisei* are great in Japan's political system, based as it is on the long-term development of electoral strongholds (*jiban*) that can be counted on to support a given politician. The allegience of a *jiban* can be transferred, so that *nisei* can "inherit" their fathers' safe seats. The *nisei* who formed the NLC were also financially independent. They had comfortable personal incomes derived from family resources and had inherited the financial connections of their fathers' *jiban* as well (Kase 1977:56-79).

That they were *nisei* moreover gave them more visibility in the Diet and in the media than comes to most junior Diet members. Kōno Yōhei's situation is of special note. Elected for the first time in Novemember 1967, Kōno joined his father's former faction, headed by his father's successor, Nakasone Yasuhiro. This situation, in which the natural heir of a famous politician came under the care and tutelage of the same politician's political heir, brought thirty-year-old Kōno Yōhei far more than the usual share of media attention. As *nisei* inheriting safe seats, Kōno, Yamaguchi, and Nishioka ran successfully for the Diet for the first time while quite young by Japanese standards. Whereas most Diet members who were forty and under were serving a first or, in a few cases, a second term, the three were far more advanced in terms of political age. But their political experience had few immediate payoffs; under the system, they still had to stand at the end of the queue. Thus, among the thirty Diet members who were "third-termers" in 1976, Kōno and Yamaguchi, as the two youngest among them, were last in line. Similarly, Nishioka, among the "fourth-termers," was third from the end in a group of thirty-three.

Kōno, Yamaguchi, and Nishioka, compared to other junior men in the LDP, had less to lose, therefore, from a conflict with their seniors. Having safe seats (with predictable campaign costs) and relative financial independence, their need for factional funds was less pressing than that of an average young Diet member trying to build a political base from the ground up. Nor did the three need to rely on the LDP's endorsement at election time. Kōno is a case in point. In his first electoral try, carrying his father's name, Kōno ran first among the candidates elected in his five-member district. From the outset, his dependency on the LDP was minimal. Being *nisei* also probably reduced these men's psychological reliance on factional ties. Media attention gave them visibility and independent identity, and their families' political connections almost certainly made them less dependent on the factions as a way of relating to the party.

Finally, the reward of future posts for accepting the LDP's status hierarchy must have been seen with particular ambivalence by these three. Whereas most young Diet members (unknown and with few political and financial resources of their own) see meticulous service to the faction as the only route for attaining leadership posts, these three had little to gain from waiting. It may be added that the privileged path these "heirs apparent" had taken must surely have made the ritualized deference they were expected to display difficult, if not painful. A general's son, is, after all, in a special position to feel the humility of being a private.

Stage Three: Initiation of Conflict Behavior

In a series of moves in the 1970s, Kōno Yōhei and the men who eventually followed him out of the LDP began to challenge the party's authority structure. Kōno, like the vast majority of newly elected junior members, had quickly aligned with a faction, the one his father once headed. All who eventually joined him, including Yamaguchi and Nishioka, were also faction members.

Within his faction, however, Kōno, by his own account, soon experienced growing dissatisfaction with the way the party was run and with his own prospects. Kōno stated at the time of the breakaway, "In January 1967 I received the official approval of the Liberal Democratic Party and became a member. In the nine and a half years since then, these very basic doubts have remained like dregs in my heart" (Kōno 1976b:96).

Kōno's criticisms of LDP leadership and authority relations were directed at its most basic features. On the one hand, he objected to the way leadership was exercised within the party: to its overconcentration of power in the hands of a small number of senior men, to the lack of turnover among the top elite, to their domination of party posts, to the rivalry among the elite for ministerial positions--a rivalry impervious to influence by other party members—and to the leaders' practice of announcing decisions without explanation or reference to a coherent ideology. A charge of special interest was that a kind of perception gap divided the junior and senior members of the party, that the senior leadership's thinking was alien to those below: "There is a large wall within the Liberal Democratic Party . . . It seems to loom thick and high in front of us, blocking us" (Kōno 1976b:97). As an example, Kōno noted that in the party platform the seniors called for "the establishment of national morals," language that echoed the prewar world in which LDP leaders had been educated, whereas Kōno and his age peers would want to call for "the creation of a new ethics" (Kōno 1976b:97).

These objections attacked the closed nature of the elite and its decision-making system. On the other hand, Kōno's criticism also points out the problems followers within the party experience: the frustration and sense of hopelessness among juniors who voice objections to party policies or who call for reforms, the intolerance of dissent shown by leaders preaching party unity ("I see democracy within the party become more and more limited each day," Kōno 1976b:97), and the absence of formal channels for juniors to influence personnel selection or party policies (Kōno 1976b:94-102).

These views, according to Kōno, developed over the nine years of his party membership prior to the break. The point at which consciousness dictated action is, of course, difficult to specify. According to most accounts, the terms of factional membership from the beginning dissatisfied Kōno, who was never an enthusiastic follower in the Nakasone faction (interview with Suzuki Tsuneo, former newspaper correspondent and secretary to Kōno, May 29, 1978). Ideological differences between Kōno and Nakasone (e.g., Nakasone was considered a hawk, whereas Kōno thought of himself as a dove) and disagreement over specific policy positions (e.g., Nakasone's support for Satō's reelection as party president in Satō's second and third terms, which Kōno opposed) exacerbated his disgruntlement. Since Kōno did not depend on the financial and political benefits that normally bind junior members to factions, the only potential benefit of factional membership remaining was access to posts. But here Kōno confronted the seniors' enjoinder to wait his turn. The specific prize that Kōno, as a *nisei*, might have seen coming was succession to his father's faction leadership. But Nakasone, only forty-nine at the time Kōno joined his faction, was the youngest of the faction heads, and barring the unforeseen could be expected to control the faction until Kōno himself was well into his sixties. Succession was thus thirty years or so distant.

By Kōno's account, his first actual challenge to the terms of factional membership came in 1971 over the issue of the People's Republic of China (PRC) joining the United Nations. The Satō government, with Fukuda Takeo as Foreign Minister, was opposed to the admission of the PRC as China's sole representative, taking the position that the PRC should be admitted only if Taiwan was allowed to retain its membership status. Then Albania introduced a resolution demanding both the admission of the PRC and the expulsion of Taiwan. There was sharp debate within the LDP over whether Japan should join the United States in sponsoring a counterproposal designed to defeat the Albanian resolution. When the party seniors failed to agree over what should be done, they followed the traditional solution to such a dilemma and left the policy decision in Satō's hands. Satō then proceeded to lead Japan into an embarrassing situation by backing the counterproposal, for it was roundly defeated in the United Nations, and the Albanian resolution passed. The opposition parties immediately thereafter introduced a bill in the Diet calling for a vote of no confidence against Fukuda to censure the LDP for a foreign-policy stand that they, along with a large portion of the Japanese public and many LDP members, saw as having been mistaken. The membership of the LDP was then faced with a dilemma. Under the terms of party discipline, they were asked to stand as one behind an unpopular and failed policy. The faction heads were expected to hold the line among their followers. Kōno, who had favored a pro-PRC position all along, thus found himself as a faction member under pressure from Nakasone to vote with the party, a pressure that he steeled himself to resist (interviews with Kōno Yōhei and Suzuki Tsuneo, May and June 1978).

Theoretically, two considerations were involved in Kōno's initiating conflict behavior. The first was choosing an arena for expressing his disagreement: the faction (i.e., raising the issue with Nakasone personally or at a faction meeting), the party (i.e., going over Nakasone's head and raising the issue with the higher-ups within the party), or outside the party (i.e., in the Diet when the issue came up for a vote). The other consideration was choice of strategy: either to confront his opponents in any one of the above arenas or to use persuasion in the faction meetings or in private conversation with Nakasone or with the party elders. The ordinary conflict strategies of coercion or reward were unavailable to Kōno, since both coercive power and rewards were monopolized by those he opposed.

The strategy Kōno adopted reflects both the power relationships within the LDP and the Japanese approach to conflict. It appears that Kōno did not consider engaging in conflict behavior in the arena of the faction itself, either in a personal exchange with Nakasone or in a faction meeting, or in the arena of the party. Status-based conflicts in Japan seem to have no obvious channel for their resolution. Kōno's status as a party junior meant that neither the faction or the party sought his views. Therefore, Kōno chose the Diet as a forum. Partly this may have been because voting in the Diet was the only channel for juniors to express their views. Turning to the Diet, however, was also a way of using ideology to affirm his position in a status struggle. The faction and the party operate on the basis of the traditional norms that affirm the authority of status superiors and deny status inferiors an independent voice, but the Diet operates according to a democratic ideology guaranteeing participation in decision making on a one-person, one-vote basis. In addition, choosing the Diet as a forum allowed Kōno to oppose those in authority while technically not exceeding his rights.

Kōno had few conflict strategies available: he had no power to coerce or reward, and normal persuasive "politicking" is not acceptable behavior for party juniors. Kōno appears to have elected the mildest form of protest available to him: failure to engage in expected behavior. When the no-confidence bill was voted on in the Diet on October 27, 1971, Kōno was nowhere to be found. He and eleven other party members from various factions were absent from the Diet in what was interpreted in the media, in the Diet, in the party, and in the factions, as an act of silent protest (*Jiji Tsūshin Sha* 1972).

Kōno's stand in the case of the no-confidence vote appears to be—and is, by his account—the first occasion in which he formally and publicly challenged the party's authority over its members.[5] Thereafter, the conflict unfolded in a series of stages that led to the breakaway five years later.

Stage Four: Escalation

Several aspects of the escalating conflict are particularly significant: Kōno's developing an organizational base for protest within the party, the issues the struggle embraced, and how the tactics of the dissident juniors and their status superiors changed as the conflict escalated.

Kōno was not alone in his stand against the party's leadership on the PRC issue; a small group of men from other factions also took part in the protest. As

---

5. There are several additional issues that he notes. However, the issue discussed here is selected because it constitutes a major episode in which Kōno publicly took a position that put him unambiguously at odds with the party's leadership.

Kōno's protest developed, a more permanent organization of junior men collected around him. Among them, as early as 1972, were Yamaguchi and Nishioka, along with some other men who eventually joined the New Liberal Club, as well as some who stayed in the LDP when that final hour came. By 1973 the group founded the "Political Engineering Institute" (Seiji Kōgaku Kenkyūjo), with Kōno as its head and with an office in Akasaka in Tokyo. According to a key member of Kōno's staff, the group had almost fifty supporters in the early days (interview with Suzuki Tsuneo, May 29, 1978). Its ostensible purpose was "to observe political and economic developments and to promote the modernization of policies and policy making" (Mainichi Shimbun Sha 1975:193). Similar study groups were started during the same period by younger members of the LDP. These groups included Seirankai, with ties to the Fukuda faction; the Hirakawa Society, which was headed by Ōhira faction member Miyazawa Kiichi; Chiyodakai, with ties to the Miki faction; and the Shimpū (New Breeze) Political Study Association, headed by Kosaka Tokusaburō, but with ties to the Tanaka faction. In the escalating conflict Kōno attempted to form alliances with these groups.

In 1973 and 1974 an atmosphere of mounting crisis prevailed within the party as the government of Tanaka Kakuei attempted to cope with the oil embargo and with its own declining popularity, and as the LDP itself was engaged in soul searching over its electoral prospects. When in the fall of 1974 Tanaka's resignation as prime minister was imminent, the inner circle of LDP elders, led by Shiina Etsusaburō, age seventy-six, was considering the question of who Tanaka's successor was to be. The secretive process to select a prime minister represented many of the features of party decision making that Kōno rejected, and it was at that point that Kōno and his group initiated a major round of conflict behavior.

Their aim was to force an open election of party president by promoting a candidate of their own. Consonant with the findings of previous research on status-politics in Japan (Pharr, forthcoming), they looked for leadership for their cause among those with higher status than themselves. They turned to middle-generation LDP leaders to find a candidate for party president who was far enough from senior elite status to be sympathetic to the juniors' cause, but near enough to be a serious contender for the position. Kōno and his group approached three such men in turn in the fall of 1974. The first was Miyazawa Kiichi, then fifty-five, of the Ōhira faction, whose leading the Hirakawa Society established his credentials with junior party members. However, Miyazawa, anticipating that he might be called on to support his own faction head Ōhira if a party election were held, declined their offer to support his candidacy. The group then approached Ishida Hirohide, age forty-nine, a leader in Miki faction to which Nishioka and Yamaguchi both belonged. Ishida also declined.

A final approach was made to Fujiyama Aiichirō. Fujiyama, a senior statesman in the party at seventy-seven, was not part of the middle generation, but for Kōno's group, he was the functional equivalent. Fujiyama had been passed over in the contest for the prime ministership and his faction had drifted away, so he had nothing to lose from running. Ostensibly, the Kōno group hoped that he would be attracted to the idea of a final try for the presidency. Second, since Fujiyama had followed a nonbureaucratic route to the Diet, he was thought to be a party senior potentially more sympathetic to the cause of ambitious juniors. It is widely believed in the LDP that the ex-bureaucratic seniors (such as Kishi, Satō, Fukuda, and Ōhira) are the most meticulous observers of hierarchical rules and thus would be most critical of upstarts attempting to push ahead of others in the line; career politicians and others are thought more receptive to such maneuvering. Fujiyama, however, also declined (Mainichi Shimbun Sha 1975:185-93).

Of the three, Ishida, according to Kōno, offered the most encouragement to the group's efforts to open up the party decision-making process. Ishida suggested that "someone among themselves" consider the possibility of running for the post (interview with Kōno Yōhei, June 5, 1978). After Miyazawa and Ishida had turned them down, the group began to contemplate putting Kōno forward as a candidate. The attempt to persuade Fujiyama to run was apparently a token effort that few in the group thought would be successful; their approach to him had been delayed because he was in the PRC on party business. Before the Kōno group met with him they held a session that ran until midnight at the Tokyo Hilton. According to observers, the group's solidarity and commitment to their cause were sufficient to lead to a consensus to "put Kōno at the head as a symbol of an effort to modernize the party" (Mainichi Shimbun Sha 1975:194).

News of this meeting reached Nakasone Yasuhiro. For some time, Kōno had not been active in his faction, but Nakasone may be seen as an agent of the party's senior leadership, and having the higher status, he summoned Kōno to a meeting on Nakasone's turf. The most detailed published account of the supposed exchange between the two is as follows (Mainichi Shimbun Sha 1975:187-8; translation mine):

Nakasone: "There's talk of your running for office. I expect you to behave prudently and to cooperate. . . . If you have some thoughts to pass along to me, I expect you to say what you have on your mind. You have a great future as a statesman."

Kōno: "I'm grateful to you for your advice. I haven't decided yet if I'll run in the election or not. I'll consult with friends about it. I don't have enough time, (but) I have a sense of great crisis. It is something that I'm discussing seriously with friends."

Nakasone: "Do you have any ideas about what I should do?"

Kōno: "I guess that you'd better not come forward as a candidate. I suppose that all the 'strong men' are responsible for this crisis."

Nakasone: "Anyway, you ought to take care of yourself."

Kōno: "I'll consult with friends."

This account, written by sources sympathetic to Kōno, is clearly aimed at putting him in the most favorable possible light. We cannot know if Nakasone actually deigned to ask Kōno for political advice, or if Kōno was so bold as to accuse him openly, along with the other party elders, of having brought the party to such a sorry pass. However, it seems reasonable to assume that the meeting did take place, and that Nakasone's suasions did not resolve the men's differences.

Several days after this meeting, Kōno sought out separately others in key positions in the Nakasone faction. This was *nemawashi,* or preparatory activity, that he considered necessary because of his formal ties to the Nakasone faction, and its main purpose appears to have been to sound out the faction's leaders and to announce his intention to make a bid for the party presidency. Shortly thereafter, Kōno made the final token effort to get Fujiyama to run. After Fujiyama's refusal, according to the best available account, "the Kōno group ran about collecting votes and the endorsements of ten Diet members who (formally) recommended him, and Kōno signed and sealed an application form for the candidacy" (Mainichi Shimbun Sha 1975:188).

In the weeks prior to Tanaka's resignation on November 27, 1974, the Kōno group tried vigorously to form horizontal alliances with the other groups of young Diet members. They clearly hoped to create ground-swell support for party reform, but in the end these efforts achieved only limited success. Each group faced strong pressures to fall in line behind their faction head (or his candidate), who, moreover, would soon be distributing posts under the new prime minister. In the end, the headcount of supporters among the young was low: the Kōno group estimated that it had only forty votes. Kōno continued his bid, however, as a way of forcing a public election for the party president.

Immediately after Tanaka's resignation, the party's leadership can be said to have mobilized to squash the Kōno group. Kōno and his followers announced to Miki, who was then the front-running candidate among the elders for the party presidency, that they would make a try for the post; he made a noncommittal response. On November 28, Nakasone, through one of his faction members who was a supporter (and cousin) of Kōno's, warned Kōno that he should be careful. A member of Kōno's group was dispatched to Nakasone in retaliation that very afternoon, requesting that Nakasone not pressure the members of his faction. This exchange suggests that the most direct messages in conflict situations may be carried by third parties. But senior Nakasone faction members, following the dictum of divide and conquer, called in junior faction members in the Kōno group and applied pressure. The strategy adopted by senior faction members in these one-to-one meetings, if reports are accurate, involved what one account calls "scolding," an appropriate term in an intergenerational conflict.

At this point, however, the curtain came down on this conflict episode. Without further ado, the party's senior leadership undercut Kōno's plans by announcing what is referred to as the "Shiina decision" to make Miki the party's choice as party president and, hence, prime minister ("Jimintō no 150 nichi," *Sekai* 1976:196-208). The move stilled all talk of holding an open election to allay the public's lack of confidence in the party.

Stage Five: Termination of the Conflict

The moves preceding the Shiina decision crystalized some features of the conflict that terminated in the breakaway of the Kōno Six in June 1976. First, the parties to the conflict had been clearly identified. The 1971 opposition that Kōno and a few others expressed to the LDP position on the PRC issue undoubtedly passed as random dissidence. The protestors were individually insignificant from the standpoint of the party's elders, and they were not organized. Kōno's bid for high office, however, was conflict behavior of a different magnitude: it was organized, and it tried, however unsuccessfully, to make both horizontal and vertical alliances. To the elders, an enemy almost surely became known; Kōno and his followers had seen the full force of the party elders' power.

The episode also found both sides choosing their weapons. The Kōno group adopted a policy of attempting to forge alliances and before the breakaway made further approaches to middle-generation LDP members in May 1976 to lead their group. The strategy of the party elders also became clear. Increasingly, their dealings with the Kōno group were mediated by go-betweens. Sometimes these mediators made serious attempts to persuade the group to fall in line; at other times their scolding or hazing made light of the conflict. In fact, during the conflict and long after the breakaway, the leadership often described the dissidents with terms normally reserved for children. "Spoiled brats," "incubator babies," and "runaway girls" were all labels widely used in the leaders' statements to the media.

Conclusion

The conflict within the Liberal Democratic Party that led to the departure of the Kōno group from the party and to the subsequent founding of the New Liberal Club reveals a great deal about status-based conflicts in Japan and about leadership problems that today divide not only the LDP but also Japanese organizations more generally. A number of characteristics of status-based conflicts will now be considered along with their implications for the terms of leadership in Japan.

The first characteristic this case study illustrates is that both instrumental and symbolic goals are important in intergenerational conflicts over issues relating to leadership. The instrumental goal Kōno and his group sought was to attain power and leadership within the party—a concrete goal they had no prospect of reaching in the short term under the normal rules governing advancement within an age-graded hierarchy. For *nisei* like Kōno, Yamaguchi, and Nishioka, to wait for positions they felt themselves already qualified for was especially onerous. The symbolic goals of the group, however, were also important for understanding the conflict. As a result of ideological changes in postwar Japan, many younger people in Japanese parties and organizations today want to renegotiate the terms of the status relations linking them to their seniors. Their demands are often symbolic: e.g., the right to be consulted, even if their views are not acted upon, and other changes in status relations that involve "better treatment." In the 1970s, the wave of LDP study groups, in which younger men still tied to their factions created for themselves spheres of symbolic participation in the party, was one manifestation of these needs. The Kōno group, then, pursued symbolic goals that are widely understood and shared among the young. They, unlike most young Japanese in general and unlike most LDP junior Diet members in particular, could press openly for these goals mainly because they, with independent financial and political resources, had so little to lose.

One related point should be noted. Theorists such as Edelman lead us to expect the powerful to yield on symbolic issues or, at any rate, to manipulate symbolic rewards as a way of avoiding concrete concessions (Edelman 1964). However, the behavior of status superiors in this case of status-based conflict belies that expectation. It is true that the LDP leadership has sometimes been willing to make limited symbolic concessions, by tolerating the new study groups, for example. However, given the party's weakness in the period from late 1974 to 1976 and its need to cling to every Diet seat to keep its majority, it is difficult to see why the leadership did not go further to satisfy the symbolic needs of the dissidents. After all, allowing Kōno, with only forty votes behind him, to run for the party presidency in a public election might well have kept him and his followers in the party and would probably have improved the image of the party to boot. And yet this type of symbolic concession, seemingly so easy to grant, was not forthcoming. It appears to be inherent in the terms of traditional junior-senior relations in Japan that symbolic concessions, which inevitably involve at least a token surrender of authority on the part of the superiors, are the hardest to exact.

A second characteristic of status-based conflicts over issues of leadership and followership is the way the relative rank of status inferiors determines their strategies in the conflict. Much studied in social psychological research on conflicts in Western nations and in studies of coalition behavior, this characteristic is of central importance here. Had the Kōno group been able to secure the cooperation and leadership of some middle-generation party members, the conflict probably could have been resolved without resort to the breakaway. If Miyazawa, Ishida, or Fujiyama had been willing to assume leadership, they might have been able to use their authority as emerging status superiors to legitimize the substitution of a new ideology of interstatus relations for an old one. To put it concretely, the outcome of their leadership might well have been a public election for the party presidency that might have led to a resolution of the conflict within, rather than outside, the party.

Finally, the status-based conflict studied here demonstrates that there are few institutionalized channels for resolving such conflicts in today's Japan. Concessions and rewards are granted unilaterally by superiors; they are in no sense negotiated through channels which could be expanded by status inferiors seeking to improve their lot (Pharr, forthcoming). In the early stages of the conflict, Kōno had no recourse but to go outside the party and his faction and take the conflict to the Diet, the only arena that, through allowing juniors to vote on an equal basis, provided a legitimate channel for the expression of his grievances. In the latter stages of the conflict, Kōno, strengthened by an organizational base, was trying to create new avenues within the party itself by attempting to institute an open election. Such an election, guided by postwar democratic ideology, would have opened a channel for the renegotiation of authority relations in the party by legitimizing the participation of juniors in party decisions. The failure of Kōno and his followers to force open such a channel foreordained the breakaway. Their failure to do so foreshadows the many struggles that lie ahead in Japan for those who seek an improvement in the terms of status relations.

Reference List

Asahi Shimbun, November 12, 1979.

Coleman, James S. 1957. *Community conflict*. New York: Free Press of Glencoe.

Coser, Lewis. 1967. *Continuities in the study of social conflict*. New York: The Free Press.

Davies, Derek. 1977. Japan's great debate. *Far Eastern Economic Review* 98:20-25.

DiPalma, Giuseppe. 1973. *The study of conflict in western society.* Morristown, New Jersey: General Learning Press.

Edelman, Murray. 1964. *The symbolic uses of politics.* Urbana: University of Illinois Press.

Ekonomisuto, July 7, 1977.

Gale, Roger W. 1977. The 1976 election and the LDP: edge of a precipice? *Japan Interpreter* 11.

Hashimoto Akikazu. 1976. Kōno shintō o sasaeru kiban wa aruka: "kikentō" no konnichi teki bunseki (Are there bases which will support the new Kōno party? A contemporary analysis of the absentees). *Asahi Jānaru* 18:12-16.

Hosojima Izumi. 1976. Hoshu yurugasu Kōno shintō (The new Kōno party that shook the conservatives). *Ekonomisuto* 54:10-14.

Iwami Takeo. 1976. Kōno Yōhei: taishū mitchaku rosen wa seikō suruka (Kōno Yōhei: Will his popular strategies be successful?). *Bungei Shunjū* 54:202-6.

Jiji Tsūshin Sha. 1972. *Jiji Nenkan 1973* (Jiji Almanac 1973). Tokyo: Jiji Tsūshin Sha.

Jimintō no 150 nichi (150 days of the Liberal Democratic Party). 1976. *Sekai* 369:196-208.

Kase Hideaki. 1977. Kōno Yōhei ni aete tou, anata no kinmyaku wa yogorete inaika (May I be so direct, Kōno Yōhei? Are your money and personal connections free from soil?). *Gendai* 11:56-79.

Kōno Yōhei. 1976a. Hoshu o sasaeru tame ni saru (We leave in order to support conservatism). *Chūō Kōron* 91:193-99.

_____. 1976b. Jimintō yo saraba: Hyaku no giron yori mo mazu kōdō osore ga wareware rokunin no shinjō da (Good-bye, LDP: Let's act now, instead of having 100 debates—that is how we six feel). *Bungei Shunjū* 54:94-102.

Kriesberg, Louis. 1973. *The sociology of social conflicts.* Englewood Cliffs, New Jersey: Prentice Hall.

Mainichi Shimbun Sha. 1975. *Seihen* (Political change). Tokyo: Mainichi Shimbun Sha.

Murakawa Ichiro. 1978. *Nihon hoshutō shōshi: jiyū minken to seitō seiji* (A short history of Japan's conservative party: Liberal democratic rights and party politics). Tokyo: Kyōiku Sha.

Nihon Seikei Shimbun Sha, ed. 1956,1960,1966,1975,1976,1978. *Kokkai binran* (Diet handbook). Tokyo: Nihon Seikei Shimbun Sha.

Pharr, Susan J. Forthcoming. Status conflict in Japan: the rebellion of the teapourers. In E. S. Krauss, P. Steinhoff, and T. Rohlen, eds., *Conflict and conflict resolution in Japan.*

Shin jiyū kurabu tettei kenkyū (Thorough research on the New Liberal Club). 1977. *Bungei Shunjū* 55:92-121.

Thayer, Nathaniel B. 1969. *How the conservatives rule Japan.* Princeton, New Jersey: Princeton University Press.

Wagatsuma Sakae, ed. 1967. *Roppō zensho* (Compendium of laws). Tokyo: Yūhikaku.

Yomiuri Shimbun, March 8, 1979.

ASUKATA ICHIO AND SOME DILEMMAS OF
SOCIALIST LEADERSHIP IN JAPAN

Terry Edward MacDougall

Two decades ago the Japan Socialist Party hit the so-called "one-third barrier" of popular vote and seats for the lower house of the National Diet, which relegated it to seemingly perpetual opposition. Although it has maintained its position as the largest opposition party, its share of the total opposition vote for the House of Representatives has dropped from 70 percent in 1960 to 40 percent in 1979, and its share of the opposition seats from 88 percent to 44 percent. (The Socialists' percentage of the opposition vote and seats increased somewhat in the June 1980 elections, but their share of the popular vote fell slightly to 19.2 percent—indicating, perhaps, a bottoming-out, but not a reversal, of their longterm electoral decline.) These past two decades have seen a rapid rise of Communist support on the left and, until recently, a less heralded but perhaps more significant growth of centrist parties, particularly the Kōmeitō and Democratic Socialists (Allinson 1976 and 1979; MacDougall 1980). By the late 1970s, these developments exacerbated a division with the Socialist Party, nearly splitting it in 1977. Although the party weathered that crisis, there is still little basis for expecting it to recover the ground lost in the past twenty years.

The immediate question for the party is whether it can reconstruct itself and its relations with other parties in such a way as to be better prepared for possible participation in a coalition government. Such efforts at party renovation, in turn, may have significant implications for the electoral fortunes of the Socialists.

An earlier version of this article was presented to the Annual Meeting of the Association for Asian Studies, April 23, 1980, Washington, D. C. I would like to thank T. J. Pempel and Sharon Minichiello for comments on that and a subsequent draft, respectively, and Terazawa Kumiko for her assistance in organizing materials used for this study. Field research was supported by the Fulbright Commission, Social Science Research Council, and the Keio University-Harvard-Yenching Institute Faculty Exchange Program. I would like to express my appreciation to these organizations and to the many persons at Yokohama City University and City Hall and in the Japan Socialist Party who agreed to be interviewed or in other ways provided valuable assistance. The interpretations contained in this article are entirely my own.

The liturgy of Socialist problems is very familiar by now (Asahi Jānaru 1978; Cole, Totten, and Uyehara 1966; Gekkan Shakaitō Henshūbu 1975; Stockwin 1968 and 1969). The party is said to be too ideological, faction-ridden, and dependent on labor in the public sector and lacking in local organization, funding, administrative experience, and leadership. These problems would be difficult enough taken one by one, but when they are considered in combination or in conjunction with the fluid situation in Japanese society and politics today (Krauss, this issue), they produce what I call "the dilemmas of Socialist leadership."

I would like to focus this article on only two of these dilemmas, although I shall refer to others in passing and in the final section. The first might be termed the leadership dilemma—the limited leverage that persons in formal leadership positions may have to effect desired change—and the second the internal-external dilemma—whether and how internal unity should be maintained while pursuing a coalitional strategy. I will analyze these dilemmas from a limited but, I believe, important perspective. Using a segment of my research on Asukata Ichio—the former mayor of Yokohama who became Socialist chairman in December 1977—I will outline how this one politician has approached these problems. It is important to do so, first, because we know so little about the operational norms of opposition party leaders in Japan and, second, because the beliefs, attitudes, skills, and resources of political leaders make a difference. Although the dilemmas they face may be deeply rooted in the country's historical experience, their actions are not foreordained. Political leaders make strategic choices and are adept or feeble in developing tactics appropriate to their problems.

The reasons for focusing on the leadership and internal-external dilemmas are to be found in the political situation prevailing in Japan in the late 1970s (Krauss, this issue). A decline in the ruling Liberal Democrats' share of National Diet seats was forcing the opposition parties to consider practical coalitional alternatives. The Socialists, however, were torn between advocates of an "all opposition party" formula and those who argued for the exclusion of the Communists, seemingly the only alternative acceptable to the centrist parties. The party leadership proved incapable of holding this feud in check or of seizing the initiative from the centrists. Both dilemmas had become manifest and posed an immediate danger to continued party unity. Thus, Asukata's approach to the chairmanship in 1977 became intimately linked to these two party dilemmas. Moreover, these dilemmas are rooted in the classical Socialist predicament of reconciling principle with practice in a capitalist democracy—a predicament exacerbated by perpetual opposition which contributes to the maintenance of a revolutionary rhetoric and ideological line entirely out of synchronization with the party's moderate activities as an established and often effective participant in the parliamentary system.

What follows is, first, an analysis of authority patterns within the Socialist Party, focused particularly on characteristics of the chairmanship. Next is a summary of the crisis of 1977 used as the backdrop for drawing contrasts between Asukata and two other top party leaders. This is followed by a more focused discussion of the leadership and internal-external dilemmas. The concluding section reflects more broadly on the interrelatedness of problems faced by the Socialists as they bear on questions of leadership.

The Socialist Chairmanship

Japanese Socialists have preferred collective leadership to having a strong party leader with clearly institutionalized authority.[1] This preference is the product of a perceived necessity for compromise among the party's diverse tendencies and factions, some of which date from divisions within the prewar socialist movement. Factionalism also circumscribes the authority of the Liberal Democrats' president, but his role as prime minister makes him more than first among equals even in intraparty matters. In contrast, the Socialists' penchant for collective leadership has been reinforced by its lack of governmental authority and, hence, of the institutional imperative for decisive action, which has contributed to a more clear-cut role for the party leader in most Western socialist parties. Moreover, the exclusion of the party's left wing from cabinet portfolios in the one Socialist-led coalition government of 1947-48 made its members, who have dominated the party ever since, particularly suspect of too great a concentration of authority. And the Socialists' ideal of party democracy has meant that its top leadership must appear to be responsive to both the party's rank and file, who exercise considerable influence through the annual party congress, and the real collective leadership in the Central Executive Committee (CEC).

The CEC, which currently numbers twenty-seven persons, is selected every other year at the party congress. It consists of a "top leadership" (made up of the chairman, secretary general and two to four vice chairmen), twelve persons who head the functional bureaus of the party, the heads of the Policy Deliberations, Finance, Election, and Diet Policy councils, and (since 1977) two persons appointed by the chairman as his personal assistants. In the past, CEC posts were

---

1. This analysis of authority patterns is based largely on discussions with officials at Socialist Central Headquarters but has been checked against such standard sources as Cole, Totten, and Uyehara 1966, and Nihon Shakaitō Henshūbu 1975. Useful interviews and informal consultations and discussions were conducted over a number of years, but I have chosen in most cases not to cite specific interviews, especially when the interpretations are based on a wide range of interviews and documentary sources. The party's semiweekly paper, *Shakai shimpō*, as well as the mass circulation *Asahi shimbun* and *Yomiuri shimbun* have been very helpful.

reserved for Diet members, but since the early 1960s an increasing number have gone to career party officials from Central Headquarters, indicating growing respect for their expertise and an elevation of their influence within the party. Most posts go uncontested and represent, instead, tradeoffs among party leaders— the incumbent top leadership, leaders of various factions or, in more recent years, study groups, and party elders. Party congress delegates, however, become the arbiters of those few, sometimes key, posts inevitably contested by one group or another in an attempt to enhance its influence. The most intensive bargaining and efforts at coalition building among groups occur with the selection of a new chairman or secretary general, although, as will be detailed below, one of Asukata's first reform proposals was the creation of a different basis of selection for the chairman, in part to avoid involving him in such "unseemly factional struggles."

The CEC formulates and publicizes party policy, presents draft annual Action Programs (*ūndo hōshin*) and proposals for revision of party regulations (*kiyaku*) or platform (*kōryō*) to the party congress, controls the organization and personnel of Central Headquarters, and communicates with various party groups through conferences of National Diet members, prefectural secretaries general, and the like. It meets at least once a week, but working groups within the CEC meet more frequently. Decisions are made by a majority vote, although strenuous efforts are made to achieve unanimity. The authority of the party's top leadership to break frequent deadlocks within the CEC was another early objective of Asukata's reform efforts.

The party congress is the highest decision-making organ of the Socialist Party. It decides broad policy directions and is the final arbiter of proposed changes in party regulations and platform. And it selects the members of the CEC, Control Commission—which inspects party organizations, disciplines members, and serves as the party's highest court next to the party congress itself- -and the Central Committee, which has become little more than a national liaison conference of party activists meeting two or three times a year. The relationship between the party leadership and party congress is the ultimate basis of legitimacy of the former and of the claim to party democracy. Delegates to the party congress are chosen according to specified ratios for local branches, federations of branches, and prefectural federations. So concerned has the party been with its claim to inner democracy that between 1962 and 1977 Socialist Diet members could attend the party congress as delegates only if selected to do so by their respective federations.

The chairman of the CEC is the party's symbolic head and most influential leader. In addition to representing the party on various occasions, from standing as its candidate for prime minister to addressing the annual meetings of major support groups (especially organized labor), he meets and negotiates with leaders of support groups and other parties, discusses and decides policy and, on occasion, parliamentary tactics with his colleagues, and proposes broad directions or a vision for party development. The secretary general assists the chairman in these functions but concentrates even more of his energies on public explanations of party policy, negotiations with other parties, and internal coordination of policy. He is very much a policy man, and it is usually he, rather than the chairman, who must answer the sharp questioning by party activists at the party congress and other conferences. The role of the vice chairman is less clear, having been created only in 1964, but liaison functions within the party as well as participation as part of an inner circle of top decision makers would seem to be central, since the posts have generally gone to persons of long seniority who are well placed to communicate with various internal constituencies—formerly largely factional in character but in more recent years including local, upper house, and female members as well. All party chairmen have served earlier as either secretary general or vice chairman although there is no explicit requirement to this effect.

Only eight persons have risen to the Socialist chairmanship since the founding of the party in 1945 (Table 1). Their paths toward power and styles of leadership have been far from uniform. Some have had "fighting records" of labor, tenant, and socialist organizing and resistance to prewar authoritarianism; others collaborated with the wartime government hoping that strong state controls might ease the path toward socialism; still others entered Socialist politics in the postwar years from backgrounds in the national bureaucracy, business, or law. There have been great compromisers as well as strong ideologues among them. In some cases both qualities have been combined in the same person. These men have had a good deal in common that has provided them with credentials to lead Japan's largest opposition party—traits surprisingly similar to those of Japan's conservative political leaders. All have been *university graduates* with *long experience* in the National Diet (at least for their times) and influential party posts and have developed *large followings* within the party before becoming chairman at an average age of over sixty. Also, surprisingly for a party in which half of its Diet representatives have been labor leaders, none of the chairmen has risen through a labor hierarchy, although all have had close labor ties throughout their political careers.

But, because of the Socialists' perpetual opposition, many of these apparent strengths have turned into weaknesses. Intellectual skills have too often been turned to refinement of ideological positions in competition with other groups within and outside the party, rather than to the solution of pressing national problems. Long experience within the subculture of the political left has made communications difficult, at times, with the general public or with other nonconservative groups who may not fully share their traditions or assumptions. Loyal followings have degenerated into bitterly feuding factions, condemned by the media and supporters who feel betrayed by the party's disunity and seeming impotence. Even skilled mediators find themselves under fire for a lack of decisiveness or inability to put the party on a realistic track for dealing with the changing conditions of Japanese society. By 1977, the accumulated problems of the Socialists brought the party to the brink of disaster.

The Party Crisis of 1977

1977 was a year of crisis for the Socialist Party.[2] In the February Socialist congress delegates affiliated with or sympathetic to the Socialist Association (*shakai shugi kyōkai*), a staunchly Marxist-Leninist theoretical study group organized outside the party, virtually took control. (For the thinking of this group's leader, see Sakisaka 1975.) The Socialist Association was formed in June 1951 by non-Communist leftist intellectuals, labor leaders, and Socialist Party members to strengthen their theoretical foundations. In 1958 leadership of the Association passed from Yamakawa Hitoshi to Sakisaka Itsurō, Professor Emeritus of Economics from Kyūshū University. Under Sakisaka the Association gradually expanded its activities beyond the study of socialist theory to a more direct involvement in Socialist politics, losing in the process the breadth of viewpoints with which it had started. Sakisaka's brand of Japanese Marxism of the *rōnō* (Labor-Farmer) school became the orthodoxy of the Socialist Association.[3] He continued to insist on the inevitable impoverishment of the working classes under capitalism and on support for the socialist nations as the forces of peace, despite rapidly rising Japanese standards of living and divisions (even hostilities) among socialist (communist) nations. To many within as well as outside the party, Sakisaka's views seemed like an anachronistic apology for the Soviet model of development and Soviet behavior in the world. Nevertheless, largely because of the vigor of its ideological and organizational activities among anti-Communist leftists at a time when no effective opposition to the ruling conservatives was in sight, the Socialist Association spread its influence during the 1960s in the lower echelons of the party, among some labor unions, and in the Socialist Youth League (*Shaseidō*), which together comprise the hands and feet of Socialist candidates at election time. Association influence reached directly to the party's highest

---

2. This paragraph is based largely on interviews with members of the Socialist Party representing a wide range of viewpoints and experience.
3. Debates among Japanese Marxists in the 1920s and 1930s over the character of Japanese capitalism produced a fundamental split between the *Kōza* school, which held that the Meiji Restoration was not a bourgeois revolution but instead fixed a new form of absolutism on Japan with its social base in feudal landholders and bourgois capitalists, and the *rōnō* school, which claimed that Japan has been developing a capitalist system ever since Meiji. The former position became the orthodoxy of Japanese Communists, while most Socialists have tended toward the latter.

decision-making organ when many of these activists were selected by their federation chapters as delegates to the party congress. By 1970 Association members began to contest certain party congress elections to the CEC, as well as to influence the content of the party's annual action program. Their strength peaked in the February 1977 party congress, when they accounted for close to half of the delegates and commanded a majority on some matters.

If this activist-dominated party congress is one face of the Socialist Party, its Diet delegation is another. Like the Liberal Democrats, but unlike the other opposition parties, most Socialist Diet members come from outside the large cities and metropolitan areas. Although backed by public employee unions—whose wide distribution gives the Socialists alone among the opposition parties a national base—some private sector unions, and the small but important party organization (ca. 40,000 members), many Socialist candidates must also rely on their personal support groups (kōenkai) based on more particularistic family, community, business, social or other local organizational ties. They must often appeal beyond a leftist organizational vote to certain other important local interests or the "floating vote." Moreover, most Socialist Diet members are former labor leaders who are adept at pursuing compensatory policies for their labor or local constituencies while maintaining a more confrontational posture on matters of principle. In addition, once inside the National Diet, they are pulled strongly by evolving parliamentary norms as well as party interest (Krauss, this issue). Such conditions generally lead to more moderate political orientations among Socialist Diet members than those of the Socialist Association. In fact, in 1977 only eight of the close to one hundred and eighty Socialists in both houses were members of the March Society (Sangatsukai), the Socialist Association-oriented Diet group (Seiji Kōhō Sentā 1977).

For over a decade and a half from the early 1960s Eda Saburō was the leading symbol of this moderate face of the Socialist Party; he also became the principal antagonist of the Socialist Association in the 1970s. Borrowing the concept of "structural reform" from the Italian communists in the early 1960s, Eda and other able young Socialists attempted to challenge the doctrinaire and factional rigidities of veteran Socialist, labor, and intellectual leaders, including Sakisaka. Recognizing the vitality of reform capitalism, Eda argued that it was necessary to oppose monopolistic capitalists and their political allies by making the Socialist Party a national, rather than a class, party. Only by doing so could it pass the "one-third barrier" toward power through a parliamentary majority. Thereafter, by cumulative reform, it could bring about qualitative changes in the economic structure and secure a socialist state. He further propounded a vision of British parliamentarianism, Soviet social welfare, American affluence, and the Japanese peace constitution. But structural reformism became entangled in the party's internal struggle for positions, resulting in its acceptance as a "tactic" but rejection as a longterm strategy. After this, Eda and his supporters, who had come from various old factions, became a force for moderation in a party still enthralled with old ideological formulations, in some cases masking other interests or career ambitions.

The Socialist failure to adjust to changes in Japanese society and to build on their early near monopoly of antigovernment support contributed to a rapid erosion of their electoral base. In 1969 they dropped from 140 to only 90 seats and from 28 percent to 21 percent of the vote in the House of Representatives election. Their major losses (and also those of the Liberal Democrats) came in the country's most urbanized areas where Communist and Kōmeitō organizational efforts proved more effective in reaching the burgeoning populations and tapping their discontents. The resulting fragmentation of the opposition in the lower house led Nishimura Eiichi, chairman of the Democratic Socialists, to call for a restructuring of the opposition based on Socialist-Kōmeitō-Democratic Socialist cooperation, or even federation. As secretary general and as leader of the moderate forces within the party, Eda represented the Socialists in the ensuing consultations, which resulted in some limited cooperation among the three parties in the 1971 House of Councilors and local elections. Eda remained the principal Socialist spokesman for such cooperation even after he was replaced as secretary general. These developments frightened Socialist Association members, who were reminded of Socialist losses after the party had participated in two coalition governments with centrist and conservative parties in 1947-48 (Cole, Totten, and Uyehara 1966:3-36; Gekkan Shakaitō Henshūbu 1975, Volume 1:122-200), and precipitated (or at least intensified) their effort to capture key Central Executive Committee posts decided at the party congress. The struggle between pro- and anti-Socialist Association leaders increased in intensity during the 1970s. Finally, Eda's last call from within the party for moderate reform and centrist cooperation came during the February 1977 party congress and was met by the cat-calls of Socialist Association-related delegates. Soon thereafter Eda left the party, not so much to oppose it as to organize persons and groups discontented with the existing parties and concerned about fundamental political reform. Tragically, within a couple of months Eda had died and with him all but a small remnant of his movement (Eda 1977; Watanabe 1977:184-87).

Led by Party Chairman Narita Tomomi, the Central Executive Committee responded to these developments by reconstituting itself as a "Party Reform Committee" to suggest means of checking the widening split within party ranks. At least some semblance of unity had to be maintained for the forthcoming July 1977 upper-house election. The results of that election were indecisive. The Socialist share of the popular vote was virtually unchanged from three years earlier but was down considerably from 1971, causing a loss of seveal seats. Unexpectedly, Narita took responsibility for this development and announced his intention to resign once a new chairman could be selected, hopefully by September. The result of Narita's decision was, first, to intensify the struggle by moderates within the Central Executive Committee to devise reforms that would restrain the Socialist Association and, second, to open the question of who would lead the party. It was in this situation of party crisis that Asukata's name was floated as a possible candidate for the chairmanship.

The Reemergence of Asukata as a National Leader

Asukata was born in 1915 as the first son of a moderately well to do Yokohama lawyer and, later, local Minseitō politician. (This account is based on numerous interviews with Asukata and his close associates. For Asukata's own account of his life and career, see Asukata 1974 and 1975; two critical appraisals are Fukuda 1977 and Iguchi 1976; the most balanced attempt at a biography is Kitaoka 1978.) His early liberal views were shaped by his higher middle school years in what he recalls as the optimistic and humanistic atmosphere of Taishō democracy, as conveyed to him by his father, several friends and teachers, his own prodigious reading in the family library, and the dramatic events of the time.[4] These views became decidedly more anti-establishment by his graduation from higher middle school, when unlike his closest friends he failed to advance along a national university course, allegedly because of discrimination against his physical disability caused by childhood polio (Kitaoka 1978:202-6). Following an alternative course through Meiji University and its graduate school, he immersed himself in Western history, philosophy, and radical thought before entering the legal profession. In his capacity as a lawyer, he met Katayama Tetsu (a leader of the rightwing of the socialist movement and the party's first postwar chairman) during their common defense of labor activists.

Through his tie to Katayama, Asukata attended the inaugural meeting of the postwar Japan Socialist Party. But his real entrance into politics was at the request of Yokohama Socialists, who recruited him to run for the City Assembly seat vacated when his father (chairman of the City Assembly) was appointed as a High Court judge. They calculated that Asukata could win the bye-election by combining Socialist organizational support with part of his father's conservative vote gathered on the basis of name recognition and personal ties. After two years

---

4. Taishō democracy, which extends into the early years of Shōwa, was the era in which party-controlled cabinets and cabinet responsibility to the Diet became part of the normal political process, despite ambiguities concerning executive authority in the Meiji Constitution. It was also the beginning of universal manhood suffrage, proletarian parties, and a wide range of social movements. Liberalization at home and accommodation with the Anglo-American powers abroad were hallmarks of the time. But difficult social and economic problems internally and momentous changes on the Asian continent were already stirring discontent in military and right-wing circles and would shortly lead to the much more oppressive climate of the prewar Shōwa years.

in the Yokohama City Assembly and four in the Kanagawa Prefectural Assembly, Asukata was elected to four terms in the House of Representatives. During these years he was a member of a small left-wing group known as the Peace Comrades League (*Heiwa Dōshi Kai*), perhaps the most problem-oriented of the Socialist factions. Recognition as a possible future party leader came as a result of Asukata's prominent role in the Security Treaty debate of 1960, particularly because of his carefully prepared and reasoned interpellations and public explanations of the Socialist position (Asukata 1960:8-13).

So by 1960 Asukata, like Eda and Narita, was one of the able young Socialist Diet members seen as likely leaders in the years to come. But the three men followed quite different paths. Eda vied for influence and power at an early age by presenting a clear strategic vision of structural reformism, which was designed to overcome the Socialists' electoral impasse after 1960 by appealing to broad segments of Japan's increasingly diverse society through a gradualist approach to socialism. Although Narita worked closely with Eda in developing structural reformism as a movement and ideology, he relinquished most of the public limelight to Eda, rising to the party's top leadership in a more deliberate and less conflictual way by demonstrating intellectual prowess· and skill in managing human relations within the party. In comparison with Eda, Asukata was skeptical about the possibility of a transition to socialism through pure parliamentarianism and deeply suspicious of the bureaucratic state, whether in its modern Japanese, Western, or Stalinist form. He chose to put himself at the head of those Socialists whose reflections on the party's impasse led them to emphasize development of grass roots organization and democratization of local political processes as necessary steps in challenging the conservatives, whose overwhelming strength in local social organizations made them so formidable at the polls. (See Nihon Shakaitō 1961 for the party's formal "reflections" on the events of 1960.) Thus, in 1963 he resigned from the National Diet and ran successfully for the mayoralty of his native Yokohama, one of the country's largest, rapidly growing, and problem-ridden cities.[5]

Asukata remained as mayor of Yokohama from 1963 to 1978. During those years he turned the city into a model of "progressive local government,"[6] with

5. Asukata's decision may have involved additional factors: his responsibility to find a strong candidate for the mayoral race (since the city was also his House of Representatives district), a calculation as to his possible political difficulties nationally as a member of one of the party's smallest and most radical factions, and the opportunity he saw for making greater headway locally than at the national level against the Liberal Democrats. In any case, he came to the mayoralship with relatively unformulated ideas about city planning and management but strong ideas about democratizing local political processes.
6. In national politics, "progressive" traditionally referred to the Socialists and Communists and their supporters in the unions and among intellectuals. With the

major innovations in citizen participation, urban planning, social service delivery, and pollution control (Asukata 1965, 1967, and 1971; Asukata and Tomida 1974; MacDougall forthcoming; and Narumi 1972). Many of these innovations served as models for other city administrations and, in some cases, influenced the shaping of national policy. Asukata sought this wider political influence by organizing the National Association of Progressive Mayors (*Zenkoku Kakushin Shichō Kai*) in 1964 and using it as a forum for disseminating his ideas on "direct democracy" as a supplement to parliamentarianism and a check on the bureaucratic state. As the ranks of opposition party-backed city mayors increased rapidly in the late 1960s and early 1970s, Asukata was able to turn this Association into a kind of pressure group for reorienting the policies and strategic vision of the Socialist Party.

Asukata's successes in this endeavor were possible because of the stagnation of Japan's largest political parties during these years. Whereas the Liberal Democrats continued to push their rapid economic growth policies on the basis of a stable majority in the Diet and favorable international conditions (inexpensive fuels and raw materials, a stable international monetary system, and rapidly expanding markets), Socialists provided weak and, often, unrealistic opposition. Meanwhile, the country was undergoing extremely rapid industrialization and urbanization, producing both great wealth and serious new urban, environmental, and social problems. Local governmental officials were the first to experience the wrath of discontented urban residents and to be pressed for practical solutions to these problems. In this situation it was possible for local governments, often led by progressives, to take the lead in policy innovation, while national bureaucrats, operating in a different political milieu, followed belatedly (MacDougall forthcoming; Steiner, Krauss, and Flanagan 1980).

By the early 1970s the Socialist Party's urban policy was largely that of the National Association of Progressive Mayors, and an increasing number of Socialists were considering the feasibility of Asukata's view of a fairly decentralized socialist state—which was the antithesis of the Socialist Association's faith in strong centralist state direction (Asukata 1970). Thus, by the December 1974 party congress, Asukata's prominence as a pragmatic

emergence of the Democratic Socialists and Kōmeitō, the old conservative (Liberal Democrats)-progressive dichotomy no longer adequately reflects the dynamics of the party system or the rise of new issues. The Democratic Socialists and Kōmeitō might more accurately be termed "moderate progressives" or "centrists" and the Socialists and Communists "left progressives." Locally, the ambiguities are even greater, since most executive and assembly posts are held by independents, issue agendas vary, and various combinations of parties form to back independent mayoral and gubernatorial candidates. "Progressive local government" is used here to mean a local administration headed by a mayor (or governor) supported by the Socialists alone or in conjunction with one or more of the other nonconservative parties.

politician of proven administrative ability and fresh ideas led several anti-Socialist Association Diet members (organized into a study group known as the New Current Society (*Atarashii Nagare no Kai*)) to ask him to run for the party chairmanship (Watanabe 1977:171-76). These persons felt that Asukata would be stronger than Narita in resisting the inroads of the Socialist Association and would present a warmer human face, attractive to the growing number of uncommitted voters. Asukata listened but in the end refused, both because he would have preferred to be a candidate of unity, rather than of division, and because he was deeply involved in preparing for his election campaign in Yokohama and in recruiting Nagasu Kazuji, Head of the Faculty of Economics at Yokohama National University, to run for the gubernatorial post in Kanagawa Prefecture.[7] Ironically, his refusal turned many party moderates against him but left open avenues of contact with the Socialist Association. But he did accept a third vice-chairmanship position, which the party created expressly for him in recognition of his contribution at the local level.

By the mid 1970s national politics was out of its stagnation and had moved back to center stage. International economic problems, particularly the rapidly rising cost of crude oil, had slowed Japanese economic growth, causing financial difficulties for local government and making costly innovations difficult. In any case, by this time the Liberal Democrats and local conservatives had coopted many reform policies and proposals of the opposition, paving the way for a more substantial welfare system and a cleaner environment—although by no means fully resolving these problems. Moreover, progressive coalition making in mayoral and gubernatorial elections had become more difficult as a result of the jockeying for advantage among opposition parties after the Liberal Democrats almost lost their absolute majority in the 1976 House of Representatives election. In this situation, which put progressive local government on the defensive, Asukata called for structural reforms in the nation's medical and welfare systems (in contrast to the high-cost social welfare policies pursued by progressives in the past), pressed the Socialist Party to adopt a local government charter embodying a long-term

7. With Tokyo and Saitama prefectures and the largest cities in the Tokyo metropolitan area already led by progressive executives, Asukata hoped to "surround" the capital by capturing Kanagawa (the nation's third largest prefecture), thereby creating a base for regional cooperation among progressive executives in the nation's heartland. But, more importantly for our purposes, he was also attempting to address one of the Socialists' most difficult problems: the lack of leaders with administrative experience relevant to national governance. Asukata clearly believed that Nagasu, a highly respected economist and a principal "brain" of the structural reformism movement, could play a central role in a future Socialist coalition government. Nagasu is now in his second term as governor, with support from all parties and wings of the labor movement, and continues to be rated as one of the best "hopes" for the Socialists in the years ahead.

commitment to local institutions and expanded opportunities for citizen participation, and joined labor leaders in investigating and discussing European concepts of self-management.

In effect, Asukata had followed a path similar to that of many Euro-communists and French socialists whose long opposition in national politics had led from skepticism of pure parliamentarianism and suspicion of the bureaucratic state to interest in local politics, espousal of direct democracy or citizen participation, and interest in self-management.[8] In contrast, Eda had tried to move his party toward gradual reform, theoretically like that of southern European leftists but in practice more akin to the social democratic parties of northern Europe. Meanwhile, Narita, who chaired the Socialist Party for most of the 1970s, had to manage proponents of both these positions, which were not necessarily opposed to each other, as well as the onslaught of the Socialist Association and the challenge of many nonfaction, Socialist Diet members whose ambitions for power were whetted by the Liberal Democrats' sudden decline.

The Leadership Dilemma

Soon after Narita made the surprising announcement of his intention to resign from the party chairmanship, Asukata and his top advisors completed preparation of a long statement of Asukata's views on reforms needed to make the Socialist Party a vehicle for pursuing political power. Meanwhile, his name was discussed, along with the pro- and anti-Socialist Association choices, as a possible successor to Narita. As the Central Executive Committee, reconstituted as the Party Reform Committee, went about its business of trying to carve out a *modus operandi* that would preserve party unity while limiting the disruptive activities of the Socialist Association within the party, tempers flared, and it became increasingly apparent that a candidate from one side would not be acceptable to the other. Thus, by the time the Committee was concluding its work and preparing for the party congress in late September, Asukata appeared as the only suitable candidate. The association was willing to support him as its second choice, since he at least recognized its importance to the party; anti-association groups were generally not openly opposed, although some expressed concern about Asukata's "leanings." In any case, both sides were so consumed by the struggle

8. Asukata is the first chairman to have long and close personal ties to major European socialists such as Francois Mitterand and Willy Brandt, as a result of extensive consultation with them since the mid 1960s. This international face of Asukata was symbolized when within a week of his selection as chairman he cohosted the Socialist International, of which he is now vice president, and was welcomed by Mitterand and others as an old friend. Relations with the French Socialist Party particularly have been intensified in the ensuing years.

over the new *modus operandi* that personnel matters were put off to the last minute.

One week before the congress, on September 21, Asukata called a special press conference and, without commenting on his availability, announced three points he felt the Socialists should include in their reforms. These were abstracted from his earlier, yet unpublished, statement. They were immediately, and appropriately, termed by the mass media "Asukata's three conditions" or "Asukata's political principles." They were, in brief, (1) the direct election of the party chairman by the entire membership of the party rather than by the party congress, (2) strengthening the authority of the chairman by, first, giving the top leadership authority to break deadlocks in the CEC and, second, giving the chairman authority to break deadlocks among incumbents of those top three posts, and (3) creating advisory panels of specialists and intellectual leaders to tap resources outside the party and to make it more open to the public and sensitive to changes in Japanese society (*Kanagawa Shimbun*, September 22, 1977).

Asukata's proposal for the direct election of the party chairman was an attempt to gain acceptance of the most fundamental tenet of his political philosophy—grass-roots participation—as a guiding principle for party reform (Asukata 1967:7-47; Asukata 1977:7-13). After having become the leading national spokesman for democraticization through citizen participation, it would have been "theoretical suicide" to accept the chairmanship without some sort of approval of this political principle from other party leaders. Instead of being consumed by the party's self-defeating struggles of the past, he was attempting to set the stage for a new party agenda. He believed that applying the principle of grass-roots participation to the selection of the chairman would make party membership more attractive, rekindle a fading passion for party activities among many members, and wrest the position itself from the unseemly factional and group struggles of the party congress. He seemed to have in mind an analogy to the local chief executive. Much in the way a directly elected mayor (or governor) is viewed in Japan as representative of the city as a whole, the chairmanship might also be endowed with the symbolism of party unity by giving it alone an all-party base of electoral legitimacy.

The second point, strengthening the leadership's authority to break deadlocks, even more directly addressed the leadership dilemma. Following a period of virtual immobility in the party because of the failure of the Central Executive Committee to make crucial decisions, Asukata sought a procedure to intensify pressure for decision and consensus. Interestingly, nearly a year after he was in office and had this authority to break deadlocks, he told the author that he had not used it (interview, August 15, 1978). The effectiveness of this kind of authority, he insisted, is in its nonuse and function of forcing party leaders to take that extra step toward carving out a workable compromise. Perhaps it should be used on occasion; but it would be counterproductive if used too often, since polarization would ensue and the chairman would be called upon to make resented one-man decisions.

Asukata hoped to accomplish several things by the third point calling for greater involvement of nonparty intellectuals and other specialists in Socialist matters. The party had stagnated as a source of fresh ideas and policies because of its inadequate expertise to address the diverse and complicated problems of an advanced industrial society, reliance on organized labor whose views it tended to articulate without sufficient attention to aggregating them into a workable program, fading dialogue with the intellectual community, and continued reluctance to tap the resources of the national bureaucracy (as the ruling party does). Much of the early vitality of the Socialist Party had been generated by an active dialogue with influential intellectuals. A revitalized Socialist Party would require such involvement once again. By bringing fresh viewpoints and technical expertise into party discussions, the Socialists would be better able to keep in touch with changing currents in Japanese society and respond to them more realistically. It might also provide the impetus for revamping what most Socialist Diet members believed to be an outmoded and detrimental official ideological line. In the long run, revision of that line was crucial in providing a "programmatic screen" which could be used to set policy priorities by creating an agreed-upon basis for aggregating diverse interests. Again, Asukata's experience in Yokohama, where he had so successfully mobilized specialists within and outside his administration for developing effective and attractive public policies to cope with difficult urban problems, was a key reference point.

The first and third conditions were part of Asukata's conception of remaking the Socialist party into a "public party," "the common property of the people" as opposed to the exclusive possession of its members. This conception was developed in the August essay but was not publicly elaborated until late autumn (Asukata 1977:7-13). Asukata's attempt to redefine the boundaries of the party, an effort that was intensified later through such means as lowering the requirements for membership, had implications for leadership. On the one hand, a representation of a wider range of interests and viewpoints in the party might free the leadership from the dominant influence of limited ideological perspectives and provide it with greater flexibility. On the other hand, decision making could become more difficult by this encouragement of participation, unless the authority of leaders to decide was strengthened. Hence, the first and third conditions could not be separated from the second one.

These three conditions did not constitute a strategic program, in regard to the party's ideological line, such as Eda's structural reformism or even Asukata's espousal of decentralization and direct democracy, but were rather tactical measures to strengthen the chairmanship and develop a new conception of the party. A candidacy based on a clear strategic choice, including a decision on future coalition partners, might have split the party at that point. What Asukata wanted were levers to reconstruct and move the party. Thus, he and his advisors directly confronted the leadership dilemma by developing these three conditions, based largely on his experience in Yokohama, to help him lead the party more effectively than Narita had. He was clearly reluctant to accept the chairmanship without some genuine indication that other party leaders were willing to give him this sort of leverage on party development.

Surprisingly, Asukata's proposals were not seriously debated at the September party congress, although members of the Central Executive Committee did signal general agreement with their intent. Measures were taken, however, to limit the Socialist Association's activities to theoretical matters and to eliminate its secretiveness. The mass media in Tokyo and most congress delegates seemed to assume that Asukata would become chairman. But many people in Yokohama were convinced that if asked (and the invitation seemed increasingly tardy) he would not accept it, given the party's failure to provide him with the leverage he had requested. This difference in perspective came out in the Yokohama editions of the national newspapers in the week between Asukata's statement of his three principles and the closing of the September party congress. National reporters, writing the first page stories, assumed that Asukata was seeking and would accept the chairmanship, while the local reporters, writing for the Yokohama edition, which appears in the back pages of the paper, understood Asukata's ambivalence and, in some cases, were doubtful that he would accept the chairmanship unless his three conditions were approved. The head offices in Tokyo simply would not believe what their Yokohama branch reporters told them (discussions with Yokohama reporters, September and October, 1977).

The evening before the final day of the congress, when seasoned leaders tried to work out some sort of acceptance of Asukata's proposals and appropriate accommodations for a slate of Central Executive Committee candidates to be recommended to the congress for approval, factional and group maneuvering intensified. This led to a postponement of Narita's planned visit to Yokohama to persuade Asukata to accept the chairmanship, the bolting from the party of three leaders of the New Current Society (Den Hideo, Narazaki Yanosuke and Hata Yutaka), and Asukata's announcement that he would not accept a draft (Den, Narazaki, and Hata 1977:180-87). The congress was thrown into disarray, then extended another day when the old leadership was reinstated until the congress could be "continued" in December.

In the two and a half months separating these "parts" of the party congress, Asukata went about his work as mayor of Yokohama, but also clarified his conception of the need for the Socialists to build an open public party (Asukata 1977:7-13). He argued that the Socialist Party had hardened into a mold that combined the secretiveness of the prewar illegal left and the factionalism of the legal socialist movement. It had become the exclusive possession of its members, organized hierarchically and infused with ideology flowing from factionalism at the center. Citing Nakane Chie's analysis of "the vertical society," Asukata argued that the Socialist Party had become "my home" for the committed, who were oblivious to changes in society as they engaged in their private ideological squabbles and career advancement within their own narrow world (Nakane 1970). No wonder the party was incapable of taking advantage of the burgeoning residents' movements and new citizen consciousness to restore its energy and reconstruct itself. Asukata felt that reconstruction was possible and pointed to the example of the French socialists, who had recovered to capture over a quarter of the popular vote after sinking far lower than the Japanese socialists had. He concluded with a reaffirmation that his three proposals would be a solid first step toward opening the party to the people and making it a "public" rather than a "private" property.

Meanwhile Narita worked unceasingly toward developing a party consensus behind Asukata and his reform proposals. He convened special meetings of the party's prefectural representatives, National Diet members, and Central Executive Committee and met continuously with labor and other support groups. Neither he nor anyone else sought another candidate, although at one point Secretary General Ishibashi Masashi seemed to indicate his own availability.[9] A steady stream of Asukata's longtime associates flowed into Yokohama, some urging him to accept, and others to decline, a draft in December.

Asukata's acceptance in early December was a result, first, of the party's approval of his political principles, in the form of a CEC promise to oversee revision of the party regulations at the December congress to incorporate his proposals. But in addition to this question of principle (and potentially very real political leverage), Socialist and labor leaders (especially Narita, Sōhyō Chairman Makieda Motofumi and Chūritsu Rōren Chairman Tateyama Toshifumi) helped convince Asukata of the necessity to make a positive decision at this time in order to avoid impending chaos in the labor and socialist movements.

Thus, Asukata became chairman in December 1977 and was confirmed, insofar as there was no opposing candidate, in an election open to all party members in February 1978. In addition to the three original proposals, he was assisted by another revision giving the chairman authority to appoint two persons to the Central Executive Committee. One was primarily an aide on National Diet

9. Ishibashi remains the likely successor to Asukata. First elected to the Diet in 1955 at the age of thirty, he was the youngest of the talented generation that made their mark at the time of the 1960 Security Treaty Crisis. Ishibashi is currently vice chairman of the party and heir to the Katsumata faction, which remains the most cohesive of the old (officially dissolved) factions.

matters and the other a political advisor and liaison on party affairs. Another reform, which Asukata discretely supported but did not originate, gave the National Diet members of the Socialist Party automatic representation at the party congress, up to one-third the total number of delegates. This further diluted the influence of the Socialist Association and increased that of the more moderate Diet members.

By putting forward his conditions for office and delaying acceptance of the chairmanship until December, Asukata accomplished several things that *helped address the party's leadership dilemma and strengthen his personal position as party leader.* First, he altered the institutional context and formal jurisdiction of the chairman, giving him greater real and symbolic authority. This was necessary not only to break a paralysis in decision making, but also to compensate for Asukata's disadvantage of having been away from national politics for so long. Asukata might need greater formal authority since, unlike his predecessors, he lacked a loyal following among Socialist Diet members and at Central Headquarters. A faction or personal following normally provides top party leaders with important informal communications channels and bargaining leverage. Also, the reforms promised to increase the importance of outside experts and the party's rank and file among whom Asukata did have a large following because of his pioneering work at the local level.

Second, Asukata bolstered his own stature and potential influence as party leader by gaining prior acceptance of his political principle of grass-roots participation. A strong Socialist chairman is expected to provide a political philosophy or ideology capable of unifying and directing the party (Kawakami 1968:20) Coming into office without some guarantee of support from other leaders for his political ideals would have meant abdicating his right and responsibility to set the tone and direction of his leadership. Third, gaining acceptance of his proposals was a practical step toward freeing him and his successors from the doctrinaire constraints of the past, and a key step in his approach to both reconstructing the party and building a broad progressive coalition—as will be elaborated below. Finally, he avoided being drawn into the bitter struggle being waged over the Socialist Association in September. By December, there was much stronger support for him as a unity candidate.

None of Asukata's proposals obviated the need to function as part of a collective leadership. He would still have to persuade others to actively support his program. But his chances for doing so were enhanced by his explicit concern for the leadership dilemma as he entered office.

The Internal-External Dilemma:
Party Cohesion and Coalitional Strategy

The Problem

Of all Japanese political parties, the Socialists have always faced the most acute internal-external dilemma, with differences over the question of cooperation with the Communists being the most vexing problem. Many of them have looked on the Communists as a legitimate part of "the progressive forces" in Japan and have argued for cooperation with them, despite recognized difference in ideology and rivalry within the labor movement and at election time. Some of the Socialists cite a common experience of suppression under prewar authoritarianism and on-again off-again cooperation in their struggle to prevent a reversion to such a system. Many are heir to the strong ideological arguments of earlier Socialists who were concerned with doctrinal purity and felt it necessary to engage the Communists in such debates. Others have argued for cooperation for more pragmatic reasons. Citing such foreign examples as the splintering and decline of Italian socialists and their own experience in 1949—when they dropped from 143 to 48 House of Representative seats while the Communists advanced from 4 to 35 after Socialist participation in two coalitions with conservatives and centrists—they express a fear that entering into a coalition without the Communists would lead to a watering down of reform proposals and a consequent loss of their electoral base to the Communists.

Other Socialists have looked on the Communists with deep suspicion, concerned about both their commitment to democratic institutions and their inroads into all sectors of Socialist support. In contrast to the first group, they argue that cooperation legitimizes the Communists and, because they are better organized than the Socialists, leads to Communist inroads among young or nonpartisan progressives who might otherwise become Socialist supporters. They often cite the experience at the local level and particularly in Kyoto where, after long cooperation, Communist strength has surpassed that of the Socialists. (See Krauss in Steiner, Krauss, and Flanagan 1980.) This group includes both Marxists and non-Marxists and in recent years has been led by persons like Eda Saburō and Den Hideo. Many of them have been interested in a restructuring of the opposition based on Socialist-Kōmeitō-Democratic Socialist cooperation and have joined extraparty groups, such as the Society for Considering a New Japan (*Atarashii Nihon o Kangaeru Kai*), to discuss long range objectives. Den and a few others have gone one step further by bolting the Socialist Party, forming the small Social Democratic League in 1978, and advocating cooperation among the "four centrist parties"—the New Liberal Club (a 1976 splinter from the Liberal Democrats), Democratic Socialists, Kōmeitō, and themselves.

Still other Socialists, among them Asukata, cannot be fitted neatly into either of these two groups; but the fundamental division with the Socialist Party is nonetheless real. In fact, so deeply rooted is it in the history of the socialist movement in Japan that some scholars see the real dividing line in the Japanese party system running down the middle of the Socialist Party. But this perspective should not be pushed too far. Japanese Socialists are extremely proud of their ability to bring together persons of varying views and of their leading role among the country's progressive forces in preventing a conservative revision of the peace constitution of 1947, checking any reversion toward a more authoritarian state, and guarding basic human rights. And they, rather than the Communists, have won the allegiance of the country's largest federation of labor unions. Sōhyō, the General Council of Trade Union in Japan (numbering over 4.5 million members), in fact, is a powerful force in holding the party together. For example, its threats to withhold financial and organizational support from those discontented Socialist Diet members who considered bolting the party in 1977-78 prevented all but a handful from joining Den.

Nevertheless, the perennial internal-external dilemma was exacerbated in the mid 1970s by two developments. One was the growing strength of the Socialist Association within the party. While militantly anticommunist, this group has argued for cooperation with the Communists.[10] Indeed, with the expansion of their own strength at the grass roots level, particularly within the Socialist Youth League, they expressed confidence in their ability to outcompete the Communists organizationally. What they feared most was cooptation by the center. The second was the sizable drop in Liberal Democratic Party electoral support, leading to their loss of control of many Diet committees and to a concerted effort by the opposition parties to define coalitional alternatives. These developments pulled Eda, New Current Society members like Den, and other Socialist moderates into serious discussions on coalitional possibilities with the Democratic Socialists and Kōmeitō. They saw their party increasingly isolated in the Diet, as the Liberal Democrats opted for cooperation with the centrist parties to get bills through committees and into legislation, largely dispensing with the old backstage negotiations with the Socialists (Krauss, this issue). Many felt that the Socialist Party was handicapped by a Socialist Association-supported ideology which was irrelevant to the Japanese people and the problems they faced currently at home and abroad and feared that the result would be to drive the centrist parties into Liberal Democratic Party hands, postponing indefinitely Socialist participation in government.

10. Despite characterization by party moderates and some reporters that this group "should be in the Communist Party," there are fundamental differences in theory and values between the Socialist Association and Communist leaders.

Asukata's Approach to the Problem

Asukata's approach to the internal-external dilemma is a natural outgrowth of his fundamental political beliefs and attitudes. Although internally consistent, this approach has been almost totally misunderstood by the national press.[11] Asukata had hoped for important tactical and strategic reasons to maintain, for the time being, the all-opposition-party formula for coalition government; but he was eventually forced in 1979/80 to abandon it for one based on a Socialist-Kōmeitō axis (*shakō chūjiku*) which explicitly excluded the Communists from consideration as a possible initial coalition partner. Pressure from the Sōhyō leadership and Socialist moderates and maneuvering by other opposition parties made this choice almost inevitable by late 1979 and weakened part, but not all, of Asukata's resistance to it. Nevertheless, the two years of "grace" he had engineered made the move far less divisive than it would otherwise have been. Asukata's preference for maintaining the all-opposition-party formula for the time being—and timing was at the crux of his approach—was not based on any commitment to or infatuation with the Communists or Socialist Association, but was an integral part of his strategy for reconstructing the Socialist Party and building a progressive opposition capable of providing a viable alternative to the Liberal Democrats.[12]

His approach to the internal-external dilemma can be explained at three levels. First, as a matter of priorities and tactics, he chose to focus first on the *internal* dimension of the dilemma—on binding the wounds of Socialist in-fighting and getting the party to work together once again. Any early decision on specific coalition partners would reignite the bitter fighting that had brought the party to the brink of schism. (The all-opposition-party formula for coalition did not necessarily commit the Socialists to include every opposition party but simply to consider them as possible partners.) Second, Asukata believed, strategically, that party reconstruction and coalition making should both begin at the mass level, by returning to the grass roots and, through a massive organizational effort, initiating a dialogue with persons in all sorts of occupations and regions to better grasp their real problems and discontents in contemporary Japan. Building on these contacts, the party should develop alternatives to the conservatives'

11. The national press continues to reduce many disputes within the Socialist Party to a simple Socialist Association versus anti-Association split, while more complicated factors are at play. It has also failed to grasp Asukata's sense of timing and how his instinctive leftist reactions are tempered by a pragmatic consideration of what is possible.
12. Asukata's relations with the Communists have never been good since his bitter experience of negotiating with them in the early 1960s over (abortive) cooperation in the national peace movement. Only in his final term as mayor did the Communists join the bandwagon in Yokohama. And, personal relations between him and the Communist leadership reached an all time low in 1979.

principles of social integration, which could serve as the basis for attractive new policies and party level negotiations. Moreover, the very process of reexamining fundamental assumptions in light of present-day conditions would help reinvigorate the Socialist Party. In his view, it was a mistake to believe that the conservatives could be defeated simply by attacking this or that policy or by hastily constructing party alliances. The conservatives' mode of social integration, for all its contradictions, had been sufficiently effective to generate a "false middle class consciousness" and conservatism among the majority of the people (Asukata 1979). In order to successfully challenge them, the progressive opposition would have to build a consensus around alternative principles which could appeal to popular aspirations and provide people with an *incentive for challenging the status quo*. Third, Asukata believed that it would be a tactical mistake to explicitly exclude the Communists while serious contradictions existed among the remaining opposition parties in their views of the framework, purpose, and process of coalition making. The Liberal Democrats might be able to exploit such contradictions, while pointing to the rightward movement of the opposition, as evidence of the lack of an alternative to the stability they could offer.

Turning first to the *internal dimension* of the dilemma, Asukata compared the Socialist Party to a broken glass. His first job as chairman would be to fit the pieces back together and apply the glue. If the glass were moved before the glue had hardened, it would shatter (interview, August 15, 1978). The mending operation involved several steps beginning as early as Narita's having arranged a CEC membership for Asukata that substituted more accommodative pro- and anti-Socialist Association representatives for the rather combative ones with whom he had worked. Moreover, realizing how badly their in-fighting had damaged the party's image—Socialist support was at an all time low in the polls—most members refrained from publicly feuding. "The real problem," explained one member of the CEC, "was whether members would simply sit back for a while watching Asukata perform, or whether they could be induced to make a positive effort to reconstruct the party," (interview, September 8, 1978).

Asukata tried to stimulate that effort, first, by getting party members involved in a massive program to widen their grass roots contacts and "construct a party of one million," second, by developing more detailed policy positions on a wide range of issues, and third, by channelling ideological debate into a Socialist Theory Center (*Shakai Shugi Riron Sentā*), which would actively seek the participation and advice of outside specialists. Thus, the first two years of Asukata's tenure in office concentrated on organization and policy making. Coalition making at the party level and revision of the party's ideological line were by choice put off until a later date.

After his confirmation vote in February 1978—he received 98 percent of the ballots cast by 83 percent of the party members—Asukata concentrated his personal efforts on the process of opening and rebuilding the party. The March party congress passed an action program calling for grass-roots-level debate on suggested means for constructing a "party of one million." Asukata became chairman of a committee formed in May to oversee this process and present recommendations to the next party congress. He personally led the upper echelons of the party out of Tokyo to discuss concrete steps with members of local chapters and federations of the party. Within the year he had travelled to thirty-five of the country's forty-seven prefectures to hold open public meetings on issues before the nation and local communities, as a further means of demonstrating his commitment to a more open and accessible party.

From its founding the Socialist Party has been internally divided on its self-definition as a "class" of "mass" party; since 1965 it has referred to itself as a "class-based mass party"—a symbolic anticlimax to the debate on structural reformism. Many veteran activists accustomed to an exclusive gathering of the committed, as well as some Socialist Association members whetted to a vanguard conception of the party, responded to the "party of one million" concept by arguing for an expansion of the category of "party friend" (tōyū) while continuing to require high levels of financial contributions, personal activism, and understanding of socialist theory for anyone desiring to be a regular party member (tōin). Party moderates argued for far less stringent requirements for regular membership. Asukata agreed with the latter and made a crucial decision that the main goal of party reconstruction should be to create a national party of regular members. The January 1979 party congress passed the recommendations of Asukata's committee, cutting financial contributions in half to 0.7 percent of one's income, allowing for selective participation in party activities, and permitting membership to those who could accept the Socialist Party Platform and Regulations (Kōryō to Kiyaku), while encouraging further political education afterwards.

Few believed that membership would actually reach one million in the foreseeable future. (The party, in fact, set a short term target of 100,000.) The real goal was to break the image of being a party dominated by labor and inaccessible to others, to stimulate greater grass-roots interaction between party members and their local communities, and to bring fresh ideas and viewpoints into the party. And, since the party has continued to view itself as one of the mass struggle (taishū tōsō) as well as parliamentary action, increased membership would help it participate more effectively in a wide range of local and national social movements.

It is still too early to evaluate exactly how successful this effort has been. Membership has increased extremely slowly (from 40,000 to approximately 60,000 by mid 1980); but the composition has been significantly altered, by departures as well as new entrants, away from the previous dominance of public employee union activists to a growing ratio of persons from private-sector unions and sharply increased numbers of housewives and persons from agriculture and small- and medium-sized industry (Suzuki 1980:38). Only one prefectural federation (Fukushima) split between pro- and anti-Socialist Association members, but even that has been reunified. Party members with different ideological perspectives have begun to work together once again.

Accompanying these organizational efforts were important changes in the tone, detail, and character of Socialist policy statements. The party released in February 1978 a first draft of a medium-term economic policy, which had been planned before Asukata became chairman but incorporated key elements of his approach to policy making. A group of scholars led by Ōuchi Tsutomu of Tokyo University was principally responsible for this draft. These scholars were largely from the Uno school of Marxian economists whose empirical orientation and nondogmatic approach to analysis based on the original theoretical contributions of Uno Kōzō (1897-1977) led to their emergence in recent years as a dominant force among academic Marxian economists (who occupy about one half of all university posts in economics).[13]   Thus, instead of the usual focus on the character of an idealized socialist economy, their draft suggested means of economic reform within the existing capitalist system over the next ten years. In place of references to nationalization or public management, an emphasis was placed on labor participation in enterprise management, industrial policy development, national advisory commissions, and local governmental decision making. Structural changes were proposed (1) away from heavy and chemical industries that consume enormous quantities of imported energy and raw materials and cause severe pollution and toward more knowledge- and technology-intensive industries with a greater component of the value added domestically, (2) from an emphasis on individual consumption to one on public life, and (3) for improvement of international competitiveness in certain weak sectors.   For financial reconstruction of the country's enormous budget deficit, the draft suggested establishment of a new tax on increases in land values, patching up various tax loopholes, and linking any tax reductions to a price index.   Despite some objections during a year of debate from the party's far left on the presumption of labor-management cooperation and potential for reform of the capitalist system (which were anathema to more orthodox rōnō school theorists), the policy was approved at the January 1979 party congress and published as *A Plan for the Reconstruction of the Japanese Economy* (*Nihon Keizai no Kaizō Keikaku*), a volume of several hundred pages.

13.   The best introduction to Uno's theory in English is Thomas Sekine, "Uno-Riron: A Japanese Contribution to Marxian Political Economy," *Journal of Economic Literature*, 13:3 (September 1975). Sekine has recently translated Uno's *Principles of Political Economy* (Harvester Press, 1980).

A similar change could be seen in the tone of the Socialists' annual action program, which was now shorter on ideological rhetoric and more detailed in its policy prescriptions. In addition, six "project teams" were established to study pressing issues on the national policy agenda in (1) education and culture, (2) problems of the elderly, (3) energy, (4) agriculture and food supply, (5) women's problems, and (6) foreign policy and defense. They began publishing their reports by late 1980 (*Seisaku Shiryō*, No. 172 (January 1, 1981) entire issue). This greater attention to detail and practical measures was perhaps more a result of active consultations with academic and other specialists than a result of improved grass-roots contacts, but the changes were nonetheless striking.

Finally, in order to control and shape the potentially explosive debate on revision of the Socialists' ideological line, the Asukata leadership established in May 1978 a Socialist Theory Center, with former party Chairman Katsumata Seiichi as director and Shimazaki Yuzuru, a Socialist Diet member and former professor of political science at Kyūshū University, as executive director. The CEC assigned the Center the highly volatile task of "Conducting research and studies necessary for developing more fully the party's ideological and programmatic line found in such documents as 'The Road to Socialism in Japan,' 'The Medium Term Party Line,' and 'The National Unity Platform' in light of the changing domestic and foreign situation and with a view toward the 1980s," (*Gendai Shakai Shugi Kenkyū*, No. 22 (April 10, 1981), 4). They were to submit their recommendations for revision of the ideological and programmatic line, after studying socialist and labor movements abroad, surveying analyses of contemporary capitalism, and holding relevant international symposia. Scholars from outside the party were to be brought in as regular members of the Center, which would conduct its work openly. Since this task was expected to take several years, the immediate effect of establishing the Center was to minimize open clashes of ideology. Indeed, it was only in the summer of 1979 after Asukata published in the first issue of the Center's journal his own vision for socialism in Japan (Asukata 1979)—in effect providing guidelines for the direction of the Center's work—that it began to move beyond the low-keyed "study" aspects of its mandate.

Asukata's approach to the *internal dimensions* of the internal-external dilemma reflects certain of his underlying political beliefs, attitudes, and concern for tactics, evident earlier in his three conditions for the chairmanship. He tends to be highly policy oriented, view problems from a citizen perspective, emphasize process or method as much as ends, and be adverse to exclusionist measures. The *policy orientation* comes, according to Asukata, from his training and practice as a lawyer (interview, October 21, 1977). He argues that a politician, like a lawyer, must understand the relationship of an issue to both general principles, whether ideological or legal, and underlying social conditions if he is to devise an appropriate policy or solution. This policy orientation was undoubtably strengthened by the challenge he faced as mayor of Yokohama to formulate public policies capable of ameliorating pressing urban problems. But consistently from the early 1950s, he strengthened his practice in this respect by voluminous reading and by soliciting the assistance of academics and technical specialists (discussions with former staff members of the National Diet Library and Yokohama scholars).

Asukata is also a rare *populist* among Japanese political leaders, most of whom are exceedingly statist in their approach to governance. He not only thinks of issues in terms of how they involve ordinary people, but also views the latter as the ultimate source of social and political change. His formulation of this perspective has varied over the years—direct democracy, citizen participation, self-management, a public party, etc.—as it has been applied toward new ends, but constant is a belief that socialist transformation must have a mass base and cannot be imposed simply from above. Closely related to this belief is the weight he puts on process, or *method*, as he prefers to call it. Thus, for example, his theory of democracy is one of method (*minshu shugi hōhō ron*), of people learning through actual practice how to stand up for their rights and interest, resolve differences, and resist intimidation by a bureaucratic state (Asukata 1967:34–46). To him the method of *participation* is most effective when it is *inclusive* and guided by a desire to serve social ends. Although a Marxist, Asukata does not see Japanese society as essentially conflictual (interview, October 21, 1977); but he objects strongly to the manner in which conservatives have engineered consensus, in his view excluding significant elements of society, or dissipating their ability and motivation to challenge the status quo (Asukata 1979). Asukata has a visceral distaste for exclusionist practices, perhaps because of perceived difficulties connected to his physical disability, but certainly strengthened by a breadth of personal contacts and friendships reaching far beyond the subculture of the political left.

These same political orientations are evident in Asukata's approach to the *external dimensions* (coalitional strategy) of the dilemma. Initially, he made no move to alter the all-opposition-party formula, rejecting what he called "the logic of exclusion." He argued against a specific delineation of coalition partners or the exclusion of the Communists, not only to avoid reigniting an explosive issue or solely because he desired tactical flexibility in the fluid situation at the beginning of his tenure in office, but also because he believed that the task before the Socialists was too formidable to be resolved simply by political agreements among leaders of the opposition parties. In the current situation of differing views among the parties on coalition making and its policy content, party-level arrangements would seem "like alliances among rival chieftains during the age of the warring states" and hardly constitute a persuasive alternative to the Liberal Democrats (interview, August 15, 1978). Moreover, as he forcefully argued in an address to Socialist members of both houses of the Diet on April 28, 1978, the essence of a progressive alternative—still to be based on defense and fuller realization of the constitutional principles of peace, democratic participation, equality, and protection of the people's livelihood—was being undermined by the conservative cooptation of the Democratic Socialists and Kōmeitō's flirtation with the right.

Reconstructing the Socialist Party in the manner noted earlier was for Asukata the vital first step in coalition making. Without it, the Socialists might not be strong enough to pull Kōmeitō—not to mention the Democratic Socialists—back into the progressive camp or to serve as a stable pivot of an effective coalition. Even more importantly, the process of returning to the grass roots, grasping real problems faced by people in different regional and occupational settings, and building from these a consciousness of alternative principles for social integration, which might serve as the basis for coalition making and a guide to policy formulation, would be the only way to successfully challenge so formidable a force as the conservative establishment.

In effect, Asukata emphasized the mass struggle (*taishū tōsō*) rather than the parliamentary (*gikai seiji*) dimension of the Socialist party as the route to both party reconstruction and coalition making. The appeal of this approach is deeply rooted in the party's early postwar history. When Socialists reflect on their marked growth in the first one and one-half postwar decades, they point to their ability to raise issues of central concern to the populace and to mobilize them in opposition to conservative efforts to revise the constitution and democratic order growing out of allied Occupation reforms. But with the increased diversity of popular concerns and aspirations and the diminuation of the threat of a conservative revision of the democratic political order, the organizational weakness of the Socialists made it increasingly difficult to grasp, aggregate, and mobilize popular sentiment to challenge the conservative establishment and strengthen their own electoral base (Nihon Shakaitō 1961). Thus, during the 1960s the Socialists lost their ability to offer a distinctive and realistic alternative to the Liberal Democrats who succeeded brilliantly in mobilizing popular aspirations for a more affluent life at minimal public expense. But, while the Socialists floundered nationally, progressive local government, supported by diverse political constituencies, played a major oppositional role in aggregating mass discontents with the social and environmental costs of economic growth. It thereby challenged the status quo with alternative values and public policies—moving the country, for example, from a one-sided emphasis on economic growth to greater concern for the quality of life. Returning to party leadership in 1977, Asukata tried to do what the Socialists in the 1950s and progressive local government in the mid 1960s to mid 1970s had done—establish political means by which the concerns and aspirations of significant segments of the populace could be aggregated and mobilized to challenge the status quo.

In other words, Asukata felt that a genuine coalitional alternative to the Liberal Democrats would have to be based on wide popular support for an alternative set of principles and policies around which oppositional parties could coalesce. Party-level, coalitional agreements would receive the trust and support of the people only if significant progress had already been made toward shaping a popular consensus on an alternative to the dominant conservative philosophy. Otherwise, the parties would leave themselves vulnerable to attack as being purely office seeking, rather than representing a more desired aggregation of popular interests and aspirations. In this sense, *establishing the popular legitimacy of a coalitional alternative was in Asukata's mind a necessary prior step to actual coalition formation*, which might have to await the electoral victory of such forces as would be willing to effect the substance of the change. To state in advance that Communists will or will not be included or that dissident conservatives would be welcomed or rejected would prejudice the legitimacy of the alternative and its chances of success.

The ideas Asukata put forward to stimulate public debate in preparation for coalition building focused on creating a more humane society, the internal dynamics of which would be more conducive to social well being and international cooperation than has been the case under the Liberal Democrats. They are most concisely summarized in his essay of July 21, 1979, on "The Outlook for the 1980s and the Tasks of Progressivism" (Asukata 1979), which also launched the public stage of the party's debate on how to reformulate its ideological and programmatic line. The central concern expressed in the essay is that life in Japan has become "administered" by the state and private enterprise and threatens to become even more so in the future, given the conservative establishment's penchant for manipulating public attitudes and value formation through increasingly sophisticated means of communications. He argues that the conservative establishment—big business, conservative politicians, and the bureaucratic elite—has created a system of social incentives and controls over a vertically integrated society that excessively narrows the range of public life and dehumanizes aspects of social intercourse. By its one-sided emphasis on economic growth, without sufficient attention to social infrastructure and amenities, the establishment has encouraged people to pursue their individual material well being at the expense of other social values that should be a part of a fuller human life. Moreover, he sees Japanese workers as being too easily manipulated by an enterprise-oriented system that sets up formidable barriers to job mobility and articulation of grievances, fostering instead a diffuse dependency supported by enterprise-based (rather than fully public) welfare programs. Partly by implication here (but more fully elsewhere), he advocates alternative patterns of job recruitment, worker participation in managerial decisions (and not simply in suggesting improvements in job operations), and a welfare system detached from one's specific place of employment.

Asukata does not deny the real benefits that this conservative system of social integration has brought the Japanese people but argues that, in addition to its dehumanizing thrust, contradictions in its economic rationality have led to severe domestic difficulties—for example, in acquiring urban land for public use or in environmental deterioration—and economic frictions with both the developing nations and industrial ones. To reverse past patterns of dehumanization through compartmentalization of society, he proposes processes of participation that develop independence while encouraging social solidarity. Thus, for example, he argues for a devolution of governmental authority and financial resources to local levels, an explicit focus on community building, and facilitation of citizen participation in this process. The purpose, according to Asukata, should not be to discourage individual or group egoism per se but to socialize it through processes of participation and accommodation in the pursuit of a better living environment and richer public life. Decentralization, however, must be supported by a reconsideration of the relationship between private and public sectors. Thus, for example, the housing problem should not be approached simply as one of creating more units but rather as necessitating a strengthening of public authority for city planning, land use, and regulation of land speculation. Similarly, the economic system must include greater incentives for investment in social infrastructure and development of public facilities; and plans must be developed for fuller utilization of localized resources, small- and medium-sized enterprise, and agriculture. Such a welfare and public, infrastructure-oriented economy is less likely than what he views as the conservatives' export-oriented (and import-consuming) one of the massive heavy and chemical industries to lead to accusations of exploitation in the developing world or exacerbate trade frictions with other industrialized countries. Peace initiatives and foreign policies aimed at resolving north-south and other international problems may then be more positively pursued.

Although most Socialists agreed with Asukata's mass-level approach to revitalizing the party and with his basic ideals of rehumanization (*ningen fukken*), independence and solidarity (*jiritsu to rentai*) through participation, devolution, and self-government (*sanka, bunken, jichi*), and positive peace initiatives (*heiwa no sekkyoku-teki sōshutsu*), many openly doubted whether this constituted a sufficiently direct coalitional strategy per se. It seemed like a slow and uncertain path, especially at a time when Japanese politics was so much in flux. Cooperation between Kōmeitō and the Democratic Socialists had been advancing rapidly, within the Diet, in local executive elections and the October 1979 House of Representatives election, and, finally, in an agreement of December 6, 1979, on the policy basis for a coalition government (for the text, see Shiratori 1980:228- 31). And although Kōmeitō still spoke of acting as a bridge between the Socialists and Democratic Socialists, the latter argued more emphatically for a separate political force of the "four centrist parties." Moreover, Sōhyō, which at crucial points in the past, like the debate over structural reformism, had always pulled the Socialists to the left, was now deeply engaged in discussions with Kōmeitō on closer political cooperation and with Dōmei unions, backers of the Democratic Socialists, on a unification of the labor front (Chūma 1981:160-61). Thus for the first time at a pivotal point in setting the political direction of the postwar Socialist Party its major support group was pulling it toward the center. Nowhere was this more dramatically illustrated than in discussions between Sōhyō and Socialist leaders between May and December 1979 during which Sōhyō pressure was exercised on behalf of an early decision for a Socialist-Kōmeitō axis in place of the all-opposition-party coalitional strategy.

Even before becoming chairman, Asukata had suggested that the very size of Kōmeitō and its closeness to the Socialists on so many issues made it the logical starting point for party-level cooperation that could lead to a broad-based progressive coalition (Asukata 1977; interview, October 21, 1977). He also seemed fully aware that the different electoral constitutencies of the two parties and the growing cooperation between Sōhyō unions and Kōmeitō (for example, on the right to strike of public employees) would facilitate actual cooperation between the parties (interview with a CEC member, September 9, 1980). On taking office as chairman, Asukata believed (or at least hoped) that he could pursue such cooperation with Kōmeitō without abandoning the all-opposition-party coalitional formula—a step he felt would reignite a bitter internal struggle, make cooperation among progressives at the grass roots more difficult, and still leave the opposition without a viable alternative to the Liberal Democrats. In other words, rather than making a symbolic change in the *form* of coalitional preference, he chose to develop the *substance* of party-based cooperation while pursuing his mass-level strategy for party revival and coalition building. Whether and how the form of coalitional preference should change was a matter of timing and substantive developments on both the party and mass levels.

But initially little progress was made in cooperation between the Socialists and Kōmeitō. Asukata's selection as chairman was viewed with suspicion by Kōmeitō leaders. After all, the Socialist Party had almost been taken over by its most radical elements less than a year earlier; and even though Socialist moderates had fought back to limit the activities of the radicals, they had not been able to expel them from their ranks. So Asukata's selection as a unity candidate represented for Kōmeitō (and some Socialists) less than the most desirable resolution of the Socialists' internal power struggle and left ambiguous the future direction of the party. Also, Asukata's decision to leave office as mayor of Yokohama in mid-term to devote full time to party activities irritated local Kōmeitō leaders who felt that in exchange for their endorsement during his 1975 bid for reelection they had received a promise that he would serve out the full four-year term. And Asukata's allegations of Democratic Socialist cooptation by the conservatives further complicated Kōmeitō's self-appointed role of acting as a bridge between the two socialist parties. Moreover, from the Socialist perspective, Kōmeitō's rightward shift on such issues as the United States-Japan Security Treaty, the Self-Defense Forces, emergency legislation, and a bill on imperial reign eras made cooperation exceedingly difficult. The problem was exacerbated by Kōmeitō's increasing attention to cooperation among centrists nationally and with the Liberal Democrats in some localities. But, significantly, there was no reaction within the Socialists for closer cooperation with the Communists.

Despite these initial difficulties, Socialist and Kōmeitō leaders persisted in trying to improve relations; and Kōmeitō relations with Sōhyō unions continued to warm. Asukata implemented top leadership consultations between the two parties promised earlier by Narita. He seemed to go out of his way to make the almost inevitable break between the two on nominating a successor to progressive Governor Minobe Ryōkichi in Tōkyō as painless as possible for Kōmeitō, although it proved quite costly for himself.[14] Moreover, given repeated setbacks for pro-Socialist Association forces, Kōmeitō could be more confident that behind Asukata, if not always in full support of him, moderate forces had become dominant. Sōhyō's intervention on Kōmeitō's behalf with the Socialists put further pressure on the Asukata leadership to abandon the all-opposition-party coalitional formula.

But, ironically, it may have been the behavior of the Communists themselves that finally convinced Asukata to go along with the bulk of the Socialist and Sōhyō leadership in abandoning the Communists. By mid 1979 the Communists had intensified their claim to the "the only true progressives" and by

14.   Asukata foresaw the likelihood well before the election that it might be impossible to recruit a common candidate for the position but felt that the manner of their split over the issue (kirikata) would be crucial. Thus, at the time that the Democratic Socialists and Kōmeitō were negotiating on a joint candidate, Asukata tried to work through a consultation group of Minobe supporters, including both the Communists and Kōmeitō, to recruit a candidate. Efforts focused on Tsuru Shigeto, a leading economist from Hitotsubashi University. Meanwhile, former Sōhyō Chairman Ōta Kaoru was projecting himself as a candidate.   When efforts to recruit Tsuru failed, Asukata criticized Ōta's campaign as an attempt by Sōhyō to dictate to the Socialists and turned instead to Gotō Kihachirō, a moderate Socialist and mayor of Musashino, a progressive showcase city in the Tokyo metropolitan area, quickly receiving the backing of the Tokyo federation of the Socialist Party. But because of insufficient funding and a lack of sufficient labor cooperation Gotō had to withdraw, leaving the Socialists with no choice but to back Ōta.
These efforts by Asukata appear to have been motivated by a desire to take an extra step to demonstrate his good faith to Kōmeitō, avoid a progressive candidate for the most prominent local post in the country who may have lacked a citizen orientation, and challenge the popular view that the Socialists remain wholly dependent upon labor. It was a gamble that did not pay off in terms of candidate selection and led to strong criticisms of Asukata; but it may have had some of its desired effects. Had it worked, the gains might have been immense.

the October 1979 lower-house elections were launching what the Socialists saw as slanderous attacks on them (interviews with two CEC members, September 25-26, 1980). There were at least two reasons for this offensive: (1) The Communists were trying to break out of their electoral stagnation by directly confronting the Socialists with whom they compete for white collar, unionist, and intellectual support. After a lackluster performance during the spring 1979 local elections, the Communists seem to have been seriously concerned that they might not be able to recoup their sizable drop (from thirty-nine to nineteen seats) in the 1976 lower-house elections in the upcoming general elections. (2) The Communists appear to have been reacting to the emerging consensus within the Socialist Party and Sōhyō that a decisive break be made with them. To judge from their efforts the following year to establish what amounted to an alternative national labor federation to Sōhyō, they may have been particularly concerned about the historical shift of Sōhyō leadership toward the political center.

Consequently, even some members of the Socialist Association became willing to accept a formal break with the Communists. Thus, Asukata's earlier concern that a decision to exclude the Communists might split Socialist ranks was no longer at issue. Furthermore, after a drop in Socialist Diet seats (from 123 to 107) in the October 1979 lower-house elections, and significant gains made by the centrists (based partly on Kōmeitō-Democratic Socialist electoral cooperation), the electoral argument for working more closely with Kōmeitō was strengthened. The December 1979 coalitional agreement between the two centrist parties put further pressure on the Socialists to act quickly lest they be left out of the momentum to create an alternative to single party rule. Although concerned that abandoning the all-opposition-party formula could still complicate his grass-roots strategy and be exploited by the conservatives, Asukata agreed to gamble on a new choice.

Thus, on January 10, 1980, the Socialists signed a policy-based coalitional agreement with Kōmeitō, including the historical choice to exclude the Communists from an initial, progressive coalitional government (for the text, see Shiratori 1980:238-45). As originally conceived and negotiated with Kōmeitō, exclusion of the Communists was limited to an early coalition government and was not to prejudice Socialist cooperation with the Communists in the Diet, local executive elections, and mass movements. This formulation offered hope (however slight) of avoiding excessive disruption in pursuing progressive causes at the local level. It also shifted the burden or stigma of such a break to some extent onto the Communists. Socialist leaders went through the motions of trying to avoid this eventuality. Making an analogy to the Italian situation, they tried to convince the Communists that it would take years before the public could accept full participation of the Communists at the cabinet level (interview with a CEC member, September 25, 1980). The Communists, however, rejected this logic and quickly refused to support new joint executive candidates or to work with the

Socialists in local and national mass movements. Even more decisively, they implemented plans to form what amounted to an alternative national labor federation competing with Sōhyō for the affiliation of lower–level union organizations.

The Socialist-Kōmeitō agreement was passed without opposition at the February 1980 Socialist party congress. Pro-Socialist Association delegates insisted only that it should not be construed as a first step toward a "conservative-progressive coalition" (*hokaku rengō*) including the Liberal Democrats. A resolution to this effect was approved only by a very narrow margin when they managed to pack a subcommittee meeting while moderates had let their guard down.

The relative equanimity with which this historic choice was accepted within the party would have been unthinkable two years earlier. Although it was not a choice enthusiastically supported by Asukata, the calm surrounding it was evidence of the degree to which internal dialogue and trust had been reestablished during the first two years of his chairmanship. To the extent that his methodical approach to the problem of party cohesion contributed to its ability to make a choice of coalitional strategy, Asukata had performed well the expected leadership role of party unifier. But his failure to convince others in the party's collective leadership of the wisdom of his mass-level approach to coalition making was striking evidence of his difficulties in consolidating his personal leadership base. Moreover, his continuing skepticism about party-level coalition making, without first strengthening the Socialists at the mass level and generating popular confidence in a substantive basis for a progressive alternative to the Liberal Democrats, elicited sharp criticism from within his party and did little to establish Kōmeitō confidence in him personally.

Some of Asukata's misgivings concerning the direct, party-level route to coalition making were to be realized before the year was over. Cooperation among progressives at the grass-roots level deteriorated in many areas of the country, and contradictions among the coalitional views and policy positions of the opposition parties proved a liability in the June 1980 upper- and lower-house elections, in which the Liberal Democrats regained their predominance. Far from vindicating Asukata's earlier stance, these new conditions created an even more difficult situation for the Asukata leadership, since it was forced to enter a period of active reconsideration of the party's ideological and programmatic line at a time when pro-Socialist Association elements were once again emboldened to challenge the moderates because of the party's inability to make electoral headway while moving in a moderate coalitional direction. Thus, even at a time when the Asukata leadership was preparing the groundwork (through a revision of "The Road to Socialism in Japan")   for a more moderate and realistic ideological and policy outlook for the party, it became more difficult to build on the moderate coalitional choice that the party had recently made.

Conclusion: How to Move the Party Toward Power
Without Losing Its Ability to Act as a "Checking Force"

What does the foregoing discussion tell us about leadership in the Socialist Party and about its ability to adjust to changing conditions and to make the transition toward governance? Unfortunately, only a few implications of the analysis can be developed in the space remaining. We have covered only the first term of Asukata's chairmanship. He has now just completed his second two-year term and been reelected to a third in the party's first popular election of a chairman.[15] Party moderates strongly opposed him for his "lack of decisiveness," whether in developing relations with the centrists or in revising the party's ideological and programmatic line. The media have decried his "lack of leadership." Yet his reelection was overwhelming; he received close to 70 percent of the vote against two moderate candidates. Clearly, as might be expected in a party that includes so wide a range of socialist perspectives, fundamentally conflicting views coexist in regard to what type of leadership is most desirable for the party.

The demand for a particular type of leadership is not a constant. It varies with the circumstances that an organization, party, or nation finds itself. We are all familiar with such illustrations of this point as Churchill's great popularity during wartime but his rejection by the British people as a person who could lead them in the task of rebuilding the country afterwards. The circumstances in which the Socialist Party has found itself for the past two decades is that of a perpetual opposition in a predominant-party system. It has been unable to project itself as a viable alternative to the Liberal Democrats as a governing party. This was not the case in the early postwar years when the Socialists represented for many the best hope for a more open and equitable society and for others a committed revolutionary leadership. But their chances for power faded as a result of internal schism and a changed domestic and international environment more easily exploitable by the country's experienced conservative leadership. In the process, the chief *raison d'etre* for the Socialists became that of a "checking force"—preventing a conservative revision of the peace constitution, backsliding toward a more authoritarian state, or violations of basic human rights. They also contributed substantially toward the creation of a welfare system by their advocacy of the interests of labor, the poor, and the weaker members of society and by their role in local government. Moreover, they have repeatedly raised

15. Asukata had been unopposed two years earlier, so the party decided to forego even a reconfirmation vote.

important questions of values and ethics, of social justice and human dignity, thereby stimulating reflection and debate on the human consequences of public policies and administrative procedures.

Few would deny the need for such a checking force in any democratic society, or for an influential social conscience. Yet, it is an enormous task to go from this limited *raison d'etre* (however essential it might be) to convincing broad segments of the populace that the party has the ability to grapple successfully with the complex problems of a modern technological society in a highly interdependent world. This is particularly the case since they have been out of power so long while the Liberal Democrats have presided over undeniable advances for the country. Even many ardent supporters of the Socialists sometimes despair of the possibility that they will be able to make the transition to a governing party.

Party moderates[16] are intensely impatient with the pace of change under Asukata and differ from center and left-wing elements of the party in regard to whether the Socialists can or should continue to play merely the role of a checking force. They are convinced that the party must break out of its limited oppositional role of the past and make a bid for power before the chance passes them by. Given the party's dwindling popular support and the ability of the Liberal Democrats to work with the centrists, they see no other choice. For once, they have much of organized labor on their side.

The moderates seek the type of *transformative leadership* offered earlier by Eda Saburō—a leadership willing to directly challenge old orthodoxies and to carve out a new role for the party. As discussed above, Eda had restructured lines of factional cleavage which had persisted since the prewar years by offering a clear vision of structural reform. Structural reformism did not prevail in the early 1960s for several reasons. The party and country were too close to the bitter experiences of prewar suppression and deep-seated distrust between the Socialists and Liberal Democrats that prevailed in the late 1950s, climaxing in the parliamentary crisis over the Security Treaty in 1960. A firmer stand on the level of principle, if not practice, appealed strongly to Socialists and labor unionists who had gone through these struggles. Organized labor particularly still pulled the

16. The moderates or right wing include two major "research groups": the *Seiken kōzō kenkyūkai* (Governing Structure Research Association) and the *Shakai shugi kenkyūkai* (Socialism Research Group). The former is largely an amalgam of the old Eda faction, the New Current Society, and some unaffiliated Socialist Diet members. It is coordinated by Yamaguchi Tsuruo, one of the party's most experienced parliamentary leaders. The latter is essentially the old Sasaki faction and is coordinated by Hirabayashi Tadashi. A subgroup with the *Seiken kōzō kenkyūkai* is the *Jishu kanri kenkyūkai* (Self-Management Research Association) led by Hori Masao. Additional moderates function in smaller groups or remain unaffiliated.

party toward a confrontational posture vis-a-vis the government. And Eda's challenge would have played havoc with the normally seniority-based patterns of advancement within the party. In effect, too much was at stake to accept revisionism in principle. Moreover, the singlemindedness with which he pursued his aims frightened opponents who would have preferred to resolve internal differences on a more consensual basis. Eda was a hard-nosed moderate who could be as dogmatic as the ideologues of the far left.

But Eda's efforts to transform the party left a rich legacy. He developed a large and loyal group of followers and colleagues among Socialist Diet members, Central Headquarters officials, and intellectuals who have been a bulwark for moderation ever since. Eda personally became the trusted link between party moderates and the emerging centrist parties, keeping alive the hope for creating a viable alternative to the Liberal Democrats even at a time when the Socialists were losing popular support. Some of his followers, like Yamaguchi Tsuruo and Tanabe Makoto, have provided the parliamentary leadership necessary to develop a practical basis for cooperation with these parties, thereby providing an element of trust that Asukata's tactical style tends to extenuate. And it is in the general direction that Eda articulated nearly two decades ago that Asukata is moving the party today, although in a manner inherently unsatisfying to those who seek a transformative leader.

The party's left wing,[17] and many in the center, however, are deeply concerned that if the Socialists do not retain a strong posture of resistance, they may lose their ability to check the Liberal Democrats. Although Socialists of every perspective are self-conscious and proud of the historic role that they, not the centrists or Communists, have played in defending the peace and democratic principles of Japan's postwar constitution, the left wing appears fearful that ideological moderation may inadvertently legitimize subtle shifts in conservative policies with longterm implications for these principles. One reason is their relatively greater skepticism about the development of a democratic political consciousness among the Japanese people. Thus, they turn to their Marxian tradition to sustain their vitality, understand the character of their oppression, and support their instincts of resistance.

Party leftists, including Socialist Association members and many within the Katsumata faction, appear most comfortable with the Narita type of *managerial leadership*. This type roughly corresponds to the stereotypical view of "the

17. On the left and center of the party are the *Sangatsukai* (March Society) which includes the Socialist Association, the *Seisaku kenkyūkai* (Policy Research Association) or former Katsumata faction, the *Shinsei kenkyūkai* (New Life Research Association) coordinated by Baba Noboru, and additional unaffiliated Diet members. Some members of the Socialist Research Group also might more properly be considered to be center rather than moderate.

Japanese leader" as a person of recognized ability who has served a long apprenticeship and is a skilled mediator in human relations. Narita is a graduate of Tokyo University who rose to an executive position in business before entering the Socialist Party at the end of the war and beginning an unbroken string of elections to the House of Representatives in 1947. His intellectual abilities and administrative skills were recognized from the start and were rewarded by constant selection to the Central Executive Committee, where he gained considerable experience in policy making, party management, and Diet tactics before being selected as secretary general in 1962 and chairman in 1969. He represented a break with traditional Socialist leadership insofar as he was a pure postwar politician bearing no prewar heritage and heading no faction. He had left the large Suzuki-Sasaki faction in the early 1960s to work with Eda in developing structural reformism; but he soon left the limelight of this movement to Eda, playing instead the role of mediator among divergent views within the party and managing personnel matters in a highly skillful way. Although he never formed his own faction, Narita was not without a loyal following at Central Headquarters and within the Diet membership of the party, built on the basis of personal trust developed during long years of experience as part of a collective leadership. As chairman, he put strong emphasis on following party procedures and channels and developing a consensus within. Narita's type of inward looking managerial leadership was particularly appealing to the left wing of the party, since it gave priority to existing channels and programs, where they had greatest influence, rather than to the pull of external change.

Asukata's instincts are those of the left wing in regard to maintaining its vitality as a checking force through an ideologically based posture of resistance; but he shares the moderates' concern for a realistic approach to policy and governance. Thus, he has sought to reform the party's Marxian ideology and program rather than to scrap it. In doing this, he has turned increasingly to the Unoists who, like himself, are inclined to use their ideological constructs as a means of sensitizing themselves to actual conditions rather than to postulate inevitable patterns of development (Sekine 1975). This is in keeping with his strategy of building a popular base for a progressive coalitional alternative, since both the intellectual and organizational efforts aim to identify those problems that could sustain popular demands for change at the present stage of Japanese capitalist development. Then, practical prescriptions for change can be developed without giving the impression of a rightward tide which might be exploited by the conservatives and result in a loss of the Socialists' ability to check them.

Asukata has provided the party with a *reformist leadership* that depends heavily on his skills as a tactician charting a course that could move the party toward power without compromising its principles and ability to resist. Thus, he has had to be as concerned with timing as with substance. From this perspective, his mass-level strategy for strengthening the party and building a progressive coalition could be seen as a tactic of delay until internal dialogue was reestablished, until the party could revise its ideological and programmatic line in a realistic direction with new input from intellectual circles, and until he could develop the personal following within the party necessary to carry it into uncharted waters. Such a course inevitably leaves the impression of "muddling through" but it may be the only way that Asukata, after so long an absence from national politics, can lead the Socialists and perhaps the only way that the party can reach its hoped-for destination intact. With his overwhelming reelection in the party's first direct poll for the chairmanship, he at last has the all-party base of legitimacy he sought from the start. And in the course of the campaign, he consolidated a strong coalition of center and left-wing groups who may be able to provide him with the informal communications channels and bargaining leverage he lacked earlier. Meanwhile, a "quiet revolution" (Tajima 1980) has taken place within the party with the passage in February 1982 by the party congress of "The Socialist Party Line and the Outlook on Domestic and International Conditions in the 1980s," proposed by the Socialist Theory Center as the essential guidelines for a fullscale revision of Socialist ideology and program. This document, which seeks to chart a distinctively Japanese socialism, receives its greatest support from the center and moderate wings of the party but maintains the posture of resistance essential to carrying the left wing as well, even though they may object to its rejection of all past models of socialist development. But the question remains whether even this, if it is brought to a successful conclusion, will not be too little too late.

References

Allinson, Gary. 1976. Japan's independent voters: dilemma or opportunity? *The Japan Interpreter* 11:36-55.

_____. 1979. *Suburban Tokyo*. Berkeley: University of California Press.

Asahi Jānaru, ed. 1978. *Gendai shakai shugi ronsō* (The contemporary socialism dispute). Tokyo: Asahi Shinbunsha.

Asukata Ichio. 1960. Tokenu shinampo e no giwaku, seifu kōben no soko ni hisomu mono (Unresolved questions of the new security treaty: what is hidden behind the government's explanation). *Asahi Jānaru* 2:8-13.

_____. 1965. *Jichitai kaikaku no rironteki tenbō* (A theoretical perspective on local governmental reform). Tokyo: Hyōronsha.

_____. 1967. *Kakushin shisei no tenbō* (A perspective on progressive city government). Tokyo: Shakai Shinpō.

_____. 1970. Shakai shugi to jichitai (Socialism and local government). *Shakai shugi*, No. 50:44-51.

_____. 1971. *Jichitai kaikaku no jissenteki tenbō* (A practical perspective on local government reform). Tokyo: Nihon Hyōronsha.

_____, ed. 1974. *Shiroto dangi: sannin Gerāru* (Amateur essays: the three Geralds). Yokohama: Yūrindō.

_____. 1975. *Ikiru, aisuru, katsu* (To live, to love, to win). Tokyo: Peppu.

_____. 1977. Shakaitō saisei e no teigen (A proposal for the revival of the Socialist party). *Asahi Jānaru* 19:51 (December 16, 1977), 7-13.

_____. 1979. Hachijū nendai no tenbō to kakushin no kadai (The outlook for the 1980s and the tasks of progressivism). *Shakai shinpō* July 27, 1979.

Asukata Ichio and Tomida Fujio, eds. 1974. *Toshi jichi no kōzu* (The design of city self-government). Tokyo: Taisei Shuppansha.

Cole, Allan B., George O. Totten, and Cecil H. Uyehara. 1966. *Socialist parties in postwar Japan*. New Haven: Yale University Press.

Chūma Kiyofuku. 1981. *Saha no kumon* (Suffering of the left wing). In Uchida Kenzō, Shiratori Rei, and Tomita Nobuo, eds., *Hoshu no kaiki*. Tokyo: Shinhyōron.

Den Hideo, Narazaki Yanosuke, and Hata Yutaka. 1977. Shakaitō ritō sengen, rittō no hata o mamoru (Declaration of resignation from the Socialist party, defending the banner of a new party). *Chūō Kōron* 92:180-87.

Eda Saburō. 1977. *Atarashii seiji o mezashite* (Toward a new politics). Tokyo: Hyōronsha.

Fukuda Hiroyuki. 1977. *Asukata Ichio kenkyū* (A study of Asukata Ichio). Tokyo: Shin Kokuminsha.

Gekkan Shakaitō Henshūbu. 1975. *Nihon shakaitō no sanjūnen.* (Third year of the Japan socialist party). Vol. 1-3. Tokyo: Shakai shinpō.

Horie Fukashi, Araki Yoshinobu, and Kusunoki Seiichirō. 1978. Kōzō kaikakuron to nihon marukusu shugi (Structural reformism and Japanese Marxism). In Nakamura Kikuo sensei tsuitō ronbunshū kankōkai, ed., *Gendai shakai shugi ron*. Tokyo: Shinyūdō.

Iguchi Gō. 1976. *Asukata Ichio o kiru* (Denouncing Asukata Ichio). Tokyo: Shin Kokuminsha.

Kawakami Tamio. 1968. *Gendai seijika no jōken* (Prerequisites for contemporary politicians). Tokyo: Shinjūsha

Kitaoka Kazuyoshi. 1978. *Beranmē iinchō* (A down-to-earth sort of chairman). Tokyo: Gakuyō Shobō.

MacDougall, Terry. 1980. Political opposition and big city elections in Japan, 1947-1975. In K. Steiner, E. Krauss, and S. Flanagan, eds., *Political opposition and local politics in Japan*. Princeton: Princeton University Press.

_____. Forthcoming. *Localism and political opposition in Japan*. New Haven: Yale University Press.

Narumi Masayasu. 1972. *Toshi henkaku no shisō to hōhō* (The theory and method of urban reform). Tokyo: Renga Shobō.

Nihon Keizai Shinbunsha. 1976. *Bessatsu kokkai binran* (Special edition of the national Diet manual). Vo. 1-2. Tokyo: Nihon Keizai Shinbunsha.

Nihon Minsei Kenkyūkai. 1980. *Kokkai giin sōran, 1980nen natsu-ban* (Manual of national Diet members, 1980 summer edition). Tokyo: Hyōron Shinsha.

Nihon Shakaitō. 1961. *1961 shakaitō no shinrosen* (The 1961 new line of the Socialist party). Tokyo: Nihon Shakaitō.

_____. 1965. *Nihon shakaitō 20nen no kiroku* (A 20-year record of the Japan Socialist party). Tokyo: Nihon Shakaitō.

Sakisaka Itsurō. 1975. *Shin watakushi no shakai shugi* (My socialism today). Tokyo: Isseidō.

Sasaki Kōzō. 1975. *Shakai shugi-teki teki seiken* (A socialist type target government). Tokyo: Mainichi Shunbunsha.

Seiji Kōhō Sentā. 1977 and 1980. *Seiji handobukku* (Handbook of politics). Tokyo: Seiji Kōhō Sentā.

Shioda Shōhei et al., eds. 1979. *Nihon shakai undō jinmei jiten* (A biographical dictionary of Japanese social movements). Tokyo: Aoki Shoten.

Shiratori Rei. 1980. *Nihon no seitō chizu* (Maps of Japanese political parties). Tokyo: Gakuyō Shobō.

Steiner, Kurt, Ellis Krauss, and Scott Flanagan, eds. 1980. *Political opposition and local politics in Japan*. Princeton: Princeton University Press.

Stockwin, J. A. A. 1968. *The Japanese socialist party and neutralism*. London: Cambridge University Press.

_____. 1969. Foreign policy perspectives of the Japanese left: confrontation or consensus? *Pacific Affairs* 42:435-45.

Suzuki Sumiyasu. 1980. Hyaku man tō kensetsu undō no jakkan no tokuchō (A few special characteristics of the movement to construct a party of one million). *Shakai Jōsei Bunseki* No. 4:38-40.

Tajima Mitsuo. 1980. Shakaitō ni okiteiru "shizuku na kakumei" ("The quiet revolution" occurring within the Japan socialist party). *Asahi Jānaru* October 3, 1980:12-17.

Tomita Nobuo, Hans Baerwald, and Nakamura Akira. 1981. Prerequisites to ministerial careers in Japan, 1885–1980. *International Political Science Review* 2:2, 235–56.

Totten, George O. 1966. *The social democratic movement in prewar Japan.* New Haven: Yale University Press.

Totten, George O., and Kawakami Tamio. 1965. The functions of factionalism in Japanese politics. *Pacific Affairs* 38:109–22.

Watanabe Tsuneo. 1977. Shinseiji to jōshiki (Common sense on the new politics). Tokyo: Kōdansha.

TABLE 1
Backgrounds of Japan Socialist Party Chairmen

Tenure as Chairman	Birth	University education	Previous career	Before becoming Chairman*			
				First elected to Diet	Age	Times elected to Diet	Times selected for CEC or equivalent post
Katayama Tetsu (9/46-4/50)	1887	Tokyo	lawyer/labor-tenant organizer	1930	59	4	1
Suzuki Mosaburō (1/51-3/60; 10/51-10/55 Left-wing Socialists)	1893	Waseda	journalist/party activist	1946	58	3	5
Kawakami Jōtarō (8/52-10/55 Right-wing Socialists) (3/61-5/65)	1889	Tokyo	professor/lawyer/tenant organizer	1928	63/72	5	-
Asanuma Inejirō (3/60-10/60)	1898	Waseda	labor-tenant organizer/local politician	1936	62	9	14
Sasaki Kōzō (5/65-8/67)	1901	Nihon	labor-tenant organizer/local politician	1947	64	8	14
Katsumata Seiichi (8/67-10/69)	1909	Kyoto	national bureaucrat	1947	58	9	19
Narita Tomomi (10/69-12/77)	1913	Tokyo	company executive	1947	56	10	15
Asukata Ichio (12/77-present)	1915	Meiji	lawyer/local politician	1953	62	4	3
Eda Saburō (10/60-3/61 as Acting Chairman)	1907	Hitotsu-bashi	labor-tenant organizer/local politician	1950	53	2	6

* Times elected to Diet includes prewar experience, but times selected to important party posts does not. Discrepancies in sources and very minor gaps in the data may mean slight inaccuracies in the age and times selected to important party posts before chairmanship. Kawakami served frequently in the position of adviser (komon) before becoming chairman, but he did not accept other party posts.

Sources: Shioda Shōhei et al., eds. 1979; Nihon Keizai Shinbunsha 1976; Nihon Shakaitō 1965.

JAPANESE PARTIES AND PARLIAMENT:
CHANGING LEADERSHIP ROLES AND ROLE CONFLICTS

Ellis S. Krauss

The contrast between Japanese and Western *styles* of leadership has often been a focus of study: the strong and independent leader, having the ability to implement his judgment and will forcefully, of Western tradition is not valued in Japan as much as the self-effacing organizational veteran who advances the collective interest through extensive consultations, skillfully facilitating the claims and interests of all members in order to arrive at a consensus at least partly satisfactory to all. (For example, see Nakane 1970:63-77.) This style of organizational leadership, like much else in Japanese culture, is said to derive from the traditional *ie*, representing the modern equivalent of the *mukōyoshi* (adopted son-in-law) whose expected attributes were "quiet ability, forebearance, perseverance, modesty, sensitivity and the ability to harmonize relationships" (Braden 1979:60).

Without denying that ideal leadership styles may vary across cultures, to concentrate only on these general comparative differences neglects other important aspects of leadership roles in modern Japan. Most especially, focusing on cultural style results in a static approach to leadership study, divorced from any considerations of the type of organization or group being led. Even within one cultural tradition, organizations with different goals, functions, and structure make different demands on and dilemmas for leaders. Furthermore, these specific demands and dilemmas are not constant, but change as the organization adapts to

This article is a revision of a draft paper presented to the Annual Meeting of the Association for Asian Studies, Washington, D.C., March 1980, under the title of "Roles and Roles Conflict in the Japanese Diet." I would like to thank the Fulbright-Hays/HEW Faculty Research Abroad program and the American Council of Learned Societies-Social Science Research Council's Joint Committee on Japanese Studies for funding that made possible the field research and analysis upon which part of this article is based. I am also grateful to the Bureau for Faculty Research, Western Washington University, for manuscript typing services in the preparation of both the AAS paper and this revised version.

a changing environment. New leadership expectations and demands may be created, or the balance among different types of older demands may be shifted, which in turn influences recruitment to leadership positions and the role conflicts the leader experiences.

During the last decade, much of the political environment of Japan has been transformed. In this paper, I propose to look at how this intensified for Japanese politicians the classic dilemma of legislative politics in democracies, resulting in new patterns of recruitment and role conflicts for party and legislative leaders.

The Diet and Leadership Roles: 1955-1970

Legislative bodies perform a number of functions, but primary among them is to manage conflicts, and aggregate the interests represented, among political parties. Party leaders must seek, via legislative action, to advance the interests and goals of their organizations; but at the same time, legislatures exist to encourage (and laws could not be passed without) accommodations among partisan interests. Party and legislative leaders are subject to potential role conflict between advancing their party's goals and responding to intraparty pressures, on the one hand, and the pressures to compromise with other parties to reach agreement (or at least to keep interparty conflicts within manageable bounds), on the other (see DiPalma 1973:15-16).

Legislatures vary greatly in their formal and informal "rules of the game" dealing with the partisan/accommodation dilemma. Thus, the role conflicts and expectations party and legislative leaders face also will be partially determined by these variations. First, let us look at two "ideal-typical" legislatures (for the basis for much of the following discussion, see Polsby 1975:277-92 and DiPalma 1977:25-28), and how their organization structures the partisan/accommodation problem and political leadership roles, and then compare these to the Japanese Diet for most of the postwar period.

One type of national legislature has been called variously the "majoritarian" or "arena" type. As in the British Parliament, there are strong and coherent parties, but no separation of powers between executive and legislature. The government is formed by majority-party leaders who formulate policy and by dominating their party control the legislature to secure passage of their bills. The principle of "majority rule" is strong, but the opposition parties abide by it because they have the prospect of taking power. Almost all legislative action takes place in the plenary session; committees, therefore, are relatively less important. Because decision making is centralized in party executives and because of strong majoritarian principles and party discipline, the main function of parliament is to provide an arena for public debate, where the opposition can criticize government policy and perhaps embarrass the government sufficiently through interpellation to bring about new elections and the possibility of alternation in power.

In this type of parliament, party and parliamentary roles are virtually synonymous, with leadership norms emphasizing the partisan side. Party leaders are parliamentary leaders, for example, the cabinet, "shadow cabinet," or party "whips." One becomes a parliamentary leader by advancement in one's party career, and one criteria for party leadership is ability to debate the party's cause in parliament. In short, the roles of spokesman to the electorate, of policy maker, and of influential legislator are all combined in the role of being a party leader.

Another national assembly, called the "synchronic" or "transformative" type, is represented by the American Congress. There is a "separation of powers" between executive and legislature, with the legislature having the ability to check or balance the executive. Party coherence is weak; majorities are formed only temporarily by shifting coalitions. Decision making within the legislature is complex and decentralized, with a strongly developed and influential committee system and procedures (seniority, for example) that give independent power to legislators. The legislature has the ability to transform government bills or even to initiate its own. The function of the assembly here is not just to be an arena, but to create or modify policy, and its "rules of the game" are designed not just to keep debate civilized, but to facilitate coalitions and negotiated agreements between individual legislators. Here, accommodation goals take precedence over partisan ones.

Leadership norms reflect the organizational context. In the United States, for example, party and legislative leadership are often separate; an incumbent president may be the nominal head of his party, but his legislative role is indirect. Major-party leaders may not even be in the national assembly, but hold only party posts, be former legislators, or local government influentials. To the extent that legislative leaders are party leaders, their party role derives more from their legislative role than from their party service. One becomes influential in party leadership by becoming influential in congress, for example, a commitee chairman or Speaker of the House; these have great procedural authority and influence bills in the legislative process by virtue of their positions. One criterion for political leadership roles in this type of legislature is the ability to skillfully negotiate accommodations between conflicting partisan and members' interests.

In the transformative legislature, in other words, there is great potential for conflicts within and between party and parliamentary roles. And, when these conflicts occur, the pressure for accommodation with other parties is likely to be strong and often supercede purely partisan interests. If the arena legislature tends to combine party and legislative leadership roles with the partisan dominant, the transformative legislature tends to create tensions between them with the legislative role dominant.

With the exception of the British Parliament and the American Congress, most national assemblies do not fit these two extreme models perfectly, and the Japanese Diet is no exception.   There is no question, however, that the Diet functioned from 1955 to the early 1970s more as an arena type than as a transformative type. With a cabinet form of government and a majority party, the Liberal Democratic Party (LDP), that had developed close ties to the bureaucracy, policy was initiated and formulated within the ministries, the ruling party and the Cabinet. Strong party discipline assured passage of legislation in the Diet, and parliament's main functions were merely to debate and legitimize post-facto decisions arrived at elsewhere (Baerwald 1974:139-41).

The American Occupation introduced, however, two innovations to the British parliamentary model that, in theory, should have enhanced the independence of the legislature and its leadership.   First, an elaborate and functionally organized committee system was introduced; second, the speaker and committee chairmen were given great procedural powers to set agendas and regulate deliberations (the Occupation wished to prevent minority "filibustering").   In the political context of the 1950s and 1960s, nevertheless, these innovations served to reinforce the dominance of government over parliament and party over legislator. Since the LDP held an overwhelming majority of seats, it controlled all the committee chairmanships and voting majorities on all committees in the lower house. With no seniority system and the frequent replacement of committee chairmen (often at the same time the cabinet was reshuffled, approximately yearly), no legislative leadership with influence or power base independent of the LDP was created.   The speakership essentially became an honorary position rewarding an elderly LDP leader who was expected to serve his party's interests when necessary (Baerwald 1974:88-102, 76-84).

Studies of government and opposition members' attitudes toward committees revealed that participation was regarded as having an insignificant influence on policy formulation (Kim 1975:82) and as "an exercise in futility" (Baerwald 1974:100). In effect, the committees became not autonomous bodies to initiate or revise legislation but only "subarenas" where the opposition could question the government in interpellations (especially in the Budget Committee). Speaker and committee chairmen became not an independent parliamentary leadership but merely agents of the ruling party's leadership. As in the British case, then, the Diet for most of the postwar period was primarily an arena, with executive dominance over the legislature and with party leadership synonymous with parliamentary leadership.

Two aspects of Japanese politics, however, distinguished the Japanese Diet. The first was that Japanese parties were not as cohesive as the British, but rather, at least in the case of the LDP and the Socialists (JSP), the two major actors, were coalitions of strong and organized personal-leadership factions. Thus party career advancement was based on seniority within a faction. One could not rise to party or (in the LDP) to cabinet or parliamentary leadership positions without long service and loyalty to a faction leader.

The second distinguishing aspect of Japanese parliamentary politics during the 1950s and 1960s was the stable electoral base of the two major parties, and their apparently fixed positions as government and opposition. After 1960 it became obvious that the JSP was never going to break the "one-third barrier" of seats and votes and was going to remain a perennial opposition. Also, although the LDP share of the popular vote consistently and gradually declined, the LDP's ability to retain seats with fewer votes was skillful enough that the conservatives seemed destined to rule perpetually. There was no prospect of alternation in power.

As a result, partisan interest dominated political leadership roles to an extreme degree. At least in the British case, one criterion for party advancement was legislative ability and skills. In Japan, only factional and party roles counted. The perpetual hegemony of the LDP left little incentive for leaders of either the LDP or especially the JSP to place accommodative strategies above partisan ones (see Pempel 1975). A skillful political leader during this period was defined as one who could bring about consensus *within* his own party and who could respond to the party's support groups.

As a corollary, party leaders lacked incentives or role pressures for public interparty accommodation. The standard scenario for legislation over which the conservatives and the socialists had strong ideological disagreements was a confrontation in which the JSP delayed and obstructed by any means possible, up to and including physical violence, until the LDP decided either to shelve the offending bill or to "snap vote" (*kyōkō saiketsu*) it through committee and on the floor. In the latter tactic, the committee chairman or speaker would be ordered to use his wide procedural powers to call for a sudden closure of debate and an immediate vote, then declare the legislation passed (Baerwald 1974:112-14; Kosaka 1969). This pattern of confrontation in the Diet occurred repeatedly in the 1950s and 1960s, with the most famous examples being the ratifications of the 1960 Security Treaty with the United States (Packard 1966) and of the treaty with the Republic of Korea in 1965 (Baerwald 1970).

By the late 1960s, such confrontations were taking place not only over ideologically sensitive issues of national defense, public order, and education, but also over such legislation as revision of the National Health Insurance Law and raising the fares on the national railways. In these latter cases, there were bases of agreement between the parties, but extreme partisan pressures on LDP and JSP leaders prevented them from indulging in public compromise. Instead, party leaders would secretly meet and agree in advance to have a snap-vote resolution to the passage of the bill, then have their parties stage the confrontation in the Diet (Kosaka 1965:54-55; Adachi 1974:94-96).

There were other indications too that accommodation was taking place behind the scenes. Thus, despite frequent intense conflicts, from 1967 to 1971, the Diet passed about three-quarters of all Cabinet-sponsored legislation, with the JSP supporting about two-thirds of the Cabinet bills voted on (Pempel 1975:69,74). But here too, the negotiated compromises—usually trivial concessions on wording by the LDP to the JSP to gain their support for a bill—were often achieved secretly. *Machiai seiji* (teahouse politics), in which party executives or other Diet strategists would meet in geisha houses or restaurants at night to smooth out the obstacles to a bill's passage, was the standard accommodation device during this period (Baerwald 1974:84). There developed a double game of legislative politics to handle the partisan/accommodation dilemma: use the Diet as an arena for symbolic public confrontation, but secretly negotiate in extraparliamentary settings the minimum accommodation necessary to pass legislation and keep the institution functioning.

In summary, the 1955-1970 Diet was a marked "arena" type of legislature, and its organization and Japan's political climate created intense partisan pressures which exacerbated interparty legislative conflict. Party executives were pressured principally by partisan demands and support groups. The valued leadership skills of party leaders consisted primarily of the ability to bring about intraparty consensus and, when necessary, to defend partisan principles by ordering direct parliamentary confrontation with the rival party. Given these partisan constraints, cross-party relationships and negotiating were minor considerations for party leaders, important only during the secret talks to get the Diet functioning once communication had broken down. Party executives, therefore, were expected primarily to be partisan facilitators and intraparty managers, a Satō Eisaku known for his skillful Cabinet appointments to balance LDP factional representation, or a Narita Tomomi with a reputation for party managerial skills who could keep the intense factional disputes of the JSP from ripping the party apart (MacDougall, this volume).

Party leaders dominated the parliamentary process. The speaker, the committee chairmen, and the parties' "Diet strategy" specialists—the "parliamentary leadership"—had little independent authority but rather would have to bow ultimately to their party executives' decisions and become partisan agents in confrontations with opponents. The major decisions were made by party leaders on partisan grounds and outside the Diet.

Nor was parliamentary leadership and talent at legislative bargaining a main criterion for career advancement. Intraparty accomplishments and loyal service to one's faction leader counted most. Appointment to Diet organs concerned exclusively with parliamentary affairs, like the House Management Committee, had high symbolic prestige as a culmination of one's legislative career (Kim 1975:73) but was not an important rung on the ladder to party or governmental leadership for LDP members. In general, within the governing party, any legislative skills valued were those of the "policy types" (*seichōzoku*) who could contribute to the discussion of bills within the party, and not the "Diet strategy types" (*kokutaizoku*) who merely carried out the task of negotiating with the opposition the minor procedural concessions necessary to hasten a bill's inevitable passage.

Many of these leadership role characteristics could be interpreted as manifestations of traditional Japanese values—the leader as group facilitator, the importance of intragroup consensus, interpersonal bargaining in small groups, and in-group loyalty versus out-group competition (see for example, Scalapino and Masumi 1962:6, 144-46). Whatever the contribution of cultural characteristics to these role norms, my argument is that they were also the result of the particular political climate and role expectations in the Diet in that era. As we shall see, with a changing political environment, leadership role norms have undergone a marked transition.

Changing Diet and Party Politics: the 1970s

Several major transformations occurred in Japanese politics during the last decade that have created new role demands on political leadership.

1. Changing Voting Trends and Party System

Beginning in the mid 1960s, Japanese voting patterns shifted, resulting in the decline of the two major parties, the rise of the smaller middle-of-the-road parties, and a new power balance in the Diet. In the four elections between 1967 and 1976, the LDP declined from 49 percent of the vote (1967) to 42 percent (1976) and from 57 percent of the seats to 49 percent. In the recent 1979 election, the LDP increased slightly its popular vote percentage but its share of seats remained virtually the same as in 1976. The LDP by 1979 had been reduced from a hegemonic ruling party with an overwhelming majority in the lower house to a party dependent on bringing in successful independent conservatives after the election to even maintain a bare majority. But the JSP declined too during the same period: from 28 percent of the vote (1967) to 20 percent (1979) and from 29 percent of the seats to 21 percent.

Middle-of-the-road parties that were either inconsequential or non-existent from 1955 to the mid 1960s gained support; the Democratic Socialist Party (DSP) and the Kōmeitō (Clean Government Party) by 1979 garnered almost one-fifth of the ballots cast and House of Representative seats. The LDP splinter group, the New Liberal Club (NLC), took 3 percent of the vote and 1 percent of the seats in 1979, and the now pragmatic and electorially oriented Japan Communist Party (JCP) had increased its share of popular vote to 10 percent and its proportion of seats to 7 percent (1979). Thus, in a decade, a polarized party system of a dominant rightist party and a large leftist opposition party had been transformed into a true multiparty system of five major opposition parties outstripping the government party in combined popular vote and nearly equaling it in seats.

In this *hakuchū jidai* (era of nearly equal power), pressures for accommodating partisan differences increased: the LDP now needed the support of one or more of the minority parties to legitimize its legislation, needed to build bridges to potential coalition partners, and needed to prove it deserved to remain in power; the opposition parties could now ally with each other to stymie the LDP (or could join the LDP when to their advantage), had to position themselves for future participation in a coalition cabinet while preventing isolation by exclusion from potential coalitions, and had to prove to the electorate that they deserved power.

2. The Changing Role of the Diet and Parliamentary Opposition

The new power balance in the Diet has also fundamentally altered the role of the committee system, the opposition parties, and the Diet itself. There are sixteen standing committees and a number of special committees (usually at least eight or nine in the lower house. Although committee assignments are roughly distributed according to a party's proportion of seats in the full house, a number of complicating factors affect the partisan control of committees. As Nathaniel Thayer (1976) has described in detail, an "effective majority" (also called in Japan a "stable majority") that would allow a governing party to control all committees' chairmanships and voting majorities requires more seats (271 or 53 percent) in the House of Representatives than a simple majority (256 or 50 percent). The LDP lost its "effective majority" in the 1976 election and failed to regain it in the October 1979 balloting. As a result, the opposition parties, for the first time in postwar history, controlled a number of committee chairmanships and/or committee voting majorities. In the 1978 Diet, for example, the opposition held four of the sixteen standing-committee and seven of the nine special-committee chairmanships. On four other standing committees, the opposition members held a majority of votes, even though the chairman was from the LDP. All told, the LDP controlled both the chairmanship and a voting majority of seats—the standard situation on *all* committees between 1955 and 1972—on only nine of the twenty-five committees in the lower house in 1979. In five of these nine, their voting majority depended on the chairman voting in case of a tie (Seiji Kōhō Sentā 1979:148).

The opposition parties have used their new committee strength to overturn or force revision of important government legislation. In March 1977, for example, the Local Administration Committee, on which the opposition parties had a voting majority but not the chairmanship, defeated a government proposal to reform the local tax law (Mainichi Shimbunsha 1977:73-74), and in 1979 for the first time in postwar history, the crucial government draft budget bill was turned down by an opposition majority in the Budget Committee (*Japan Times Weekly* 1979). Although these committee-rejected bills were later passed in the full house by a simple LDP majority, the mere threat of such legislative difficulty can sometimes force concessions: the government revised its proposed budget in 1977 because of the united demands of the opposition parties, only the third time in postwar history the draft budget had been revised after submission and the first time because of opposition pressure (Mainichi Shimbunsha 1977:165).

In other words, the committee system was no longer an irrelevant and largely functionless structure in the Diet but was an important site for interparty bargaining with the prospect of real revision in legislation. The opposition had new power in a normal parliamentary channel to express itself. Finally, as a result of these factors and the real pressures for interparty accommodation in the Diet, parliament and legislative politics played a larger role in the political strategies of all the parties and in the political process itself. The Diet was no longer just an arena for symbolic conflict and post-facto legitimization of policy; it was the site of real bargaining and attempted accommodation between the parties, where, potentially, policy could be affected.

3. The Rise of New Issues and Voter Expectations

New issues have become salient and new expectations and demands have arisen during the last decade, changing the context in which the parties and their leadership operate. In place of the cold war issues of national security and foreign policy, and the symbolic issues of public order and education that were vestiges of the prewar and Occupation past, issues of concrete policy have increased in importance. The LDP's almost exclusive attention to rapid economic growth after 1960 created affluence, but once it was achieved, many Japanese had less patience with the pollution that accompanied it and with the inadequacy of social services that had been sacrificed in the drive for higher GNP. These new concerns cut across the traditional political divisions of left and right and created pressure within all the parties' support networks for more emphasis on policies to improve the environment, welfare services, and the quality of life (Steiner, Krauss, and Flanagan 1980). These are issues upon which the parties can find themselves in closer agreement, and are more amenable to negotiation, than the more intractible symbolic issues of the previous era.

A new and large group of voters in Japan who are attuned to these very policy issues, moreover, has become increasingly important in winning elections in urban areas. "Floating voters" not tied to the traditional support networks of the parties have been estimated recently to comprise as much as 15 percent of the national electorate and in large metropolitan areas like Tokyo perhaps as much as 40 percent. As Gary Allinson (1976) has argued, these new floating voters are likely to be highly educated, concerned with policy issues and the ability of the parties to respond to the problems of industrialized society. There is thus greater pressure on and incentive for parties and their leadership to appear responsible and responsive.

A demand for cleaner and more open politics has also arisen, stimulated to a large extent by the mass media and also by the Communist Party, which has used dissatisfaction with secret and corrupt politics to portray itself as a "purer" alternative. In the late 1960s and early 1970s, both the media and the JCP began to severely criticize the machiai seiji practiced by the LDP and the JSP, criticism which was particularly embarrassing to the Socialists. With the Lockheed scandal and the resignation of Prime Minister Tanaka Kakuei, and then the secession of the NLC from the LDP over the necessity of party reform, the issue of corruption and behind-the-scenes politics reached its peak and led all the parties to try to present an image of being less corrupt and elitist. The LDP's introduction of a party presidential "primary" system and Asukata Ichio's championing of broadening the base of the JSP through creating a "party of one million" (see MacDougall, this volume) must be seen, at least in part, as a response to new public expectations that party leaders and party organizations become more open, both to citizen participation and in their operating style.

Changing Leadership Role Norms

These changes in Japanese politics during the last decade have affected Japanese party and parliamentary leadership roles. My evidence for these effects comes from secondary sources and also from interviews I conducted with nineteen members of the House of Representatives, three members of the House of Councilors, and an administrative assistant (hisho) to the Speaker of the House of Representatives in the summer of 1978. Respondents included at least one from all (seven) major parties. Their career backgrounds included three present or past party chairman or secretaries-general; fourteen other past or present high party posts; and twelve key Diet policy and management positions (for details, see Krauss, forthcoming).

Party Executives

The greatest change in the role of party leaders is that they had to reconcile partisan interests with the pressures for accommodation with rival parties. Party strategies in a multiple-party system with near government-opposition parity are so intertwined with and dependent upon negotiations with the other parties that no party leader can respond solely to intraparty interests. To the necessity of achieving consensus within one's party had been added the necessity of achieving consensus with other parties as well, and each task complicated the attainment of the other.

A party's position on any particular issue may affect its relations with other parties and the prospects for coalition. When the Kōmeitō, for example, reversed its position on the so-called "*yūji rippō*" (emergency mobilization of the Self-Defense forces legislation), it was also widely perceived as deciding to align itself with the leftist parties against the "center" DSP and NLC (Mainichi Shimbun 1978). Issues causing the greatest internal dissension within each of the opposition parties in recent years have not been solely the ideological or personal leadership ones, as in the past, but have revolved around the very question of coalition strategy. In the JSP the problem of coalition with the Communists or the center parties has been one of the central intraparty debates (see MacDougall, this volume). The resignation of Nishioka Takeo from the NLC ostensibly followed a disagreement with Kōno Yōhei over whether the party should move toward alignment with the center parties or cooperate more closely with the LDP (Shimizu 1979b). Within the Kōmeitō, constant pressure to align with either the DSP on the right or the JSP on the left provoked rumors of a split between Takeiri Yoshikatsu and Yano Junya on which course best serves the party's interests.

The LDP prime ministers and party executives now regularly consider opposition as well as the many intraparty interests. Instead of relying on trivial concessions toward the opposition on noncontroversial legislation and executing party will through a "snap vote" on controversial bills, the last three prime ministers (i.e., since 1976) have normally attempted to negotiate a consensus to include some opposition parties before bringing a bill to a vote. Failing this, important legislation has been deferred. For example, failing to gain enough opposition support for the Non-Proliferation Treaty in the 1975 session, Prime Minister Miki Takeo put it off until the next session where such support could be achieved (Endicott 1977:286-88).

Even a supposedly "hawkish" leader like Fukuda Takeo conformed to these new norms, approving informal revision of the government's budget rather than force it through over the demands of the united opposition parties for the bill's revision and a tax cut. He took this almost unprecedented step despite the fact that opposition to revision was initially widespread in the LDP and the bureaucracy. The party's Executive Council, however, left the door open to negotiations providing the three top party leaders assumed responsibility. Prime Minister Fukuda and the others agreed to entrust the negotiations to Secretary General Ōhira Masayashi, who proceeded to hammer out a compromise (Mainichi Shimbunsha 1977:154-69).

After Ōhira became prime minister, the practice of passing legislation with opposition support has been formalized in his famous "*bubun rengō*" strategy of "partial coalition": even without formal participation of other parties in the Cabinet, the government will negotiate coalitions on specific bills with the opposition parties. These new norms of party and legislative leadership have restrained parliamentary confrontations; since 1976, there has been only one "snap vote" in the Diet (on the Continental Shelf Treaty with the Republic of Korea).

LDP leaders still confront the dilemma of satisfying both intractible intraparty interests, which may jeopardize one's leadership, and the need to accommodate the opposition parties, to prevent the sacrifice of more general party and national goals. A compromise, as over the 1977 budget, may not always be available. A skillful leader may have to attempt to satisfy each side serially, or play one against the other. A close political lieutenant of Ōhira's, who subsequently went on to an important Cabinet-related post, told me in 1978 that balancing opposition demands for budget revision with intraparty resistance to it might well require a strategy of satisfying the opposition and the party in alternate years—accepting some revision one year, holding fast against it the next. During the maneuvering before the unprecedented split LDP parliamentary vote in late 1979 reelecting Ōhira as prime minister, Ōhira offered the NLC a cabinet post, knowing such action would not be acceptable to the party; the gesture secured NLC support in the vote for prime minister (Shimizu 1979c).

The role of party leader in making legislative accommodations with rival parties has become increasingly specialized, public, and formalized. My interviews revealed that secret *machiai seiji* has drastically declined, and interparty negotiations have taken on a defined and more institutionalized pattern. Most legislative negotiations between government and opposition take place at lower and intermediate levels of party and parliamentary leadership, particularly in the meetings of the directors (*Riji*; the executive committee, in effect) of the House Management (Steering) Committee and other committees. If such negotiations reach an impasse, the problem is handed over to a meeting of the parties' Diet Policy Committee chairmen. These negotiations at lower and intermediate levels more frequently than not now take place within the Diet building or in the Diet members' offices. If agreement is not reached on a major issue, then the party leaders, chairmen and/or secretaries-general, may meet to try to break the impasse. Nowadays, the occurrence of these meetings is publicized, with media coverage of the arrival and departure of the executives. This is not to say that prior, covert, and informal contacts have completely disappeared in Japanese politics, only that *machiai seiji* of top leaders is no longer the major form of partisan negotiation.

There are probably two reasons for this development. One is certainly that public criticism of behind-the-scenes deals and the demand for more "open" politics made all the parties attempt to find alternative forms of contact. But there is also a more practical reason: resolving issues between government and opposition by the informal meeting of party leaders is simpler when there are only two parties involved. In the multiparty age, as a number of my respondents indicated, the complex negotiations that must take place require more formalized and institutionalized mechanisms. It is simply too complicated to reach legislative accommodation today solely by secret bilateral meetings of party leaders.

Parliamentary Leadership

Managing legislation in the Diet is largely the responsibility of the Speaker of the House, the House Management Committee (Giin Un'ei Iinkai), and each party's Diet Policy Committee (Kokkai Taisaku Iinkai). The speaker's ultimate duty is to ensure the smooth conduct of legislative business; the House Management Committee is a steering committee handling daily procedural business involving legislation, and unlike other committees is not concerned with deliberating the content of bills. The overall legislative strategy of each party focuses there, and key battles are fought over parliamentary procedures determining each stage of a bill's passage through the House (see Baerwald 1974:84).

The House Management Committee's decisions are in fact not made by the whole committee of twenty-five members, but rather by the smaller group of the chairman and the committee *Riji* constituting its executive committee, which meets daily when the Diet is in session. (The full committee nearly always unanimously approves decisions taken by its executive committee.) The chairman is usually a veteran LDP politician trusted by the speaker, with whom he stays in close contact. Parties with more than twenty representatives in the House will be allocated *Riji* posts in rough proportion to their Diet strength. This key parliamentary body is linked to the parties' Diet Policy Committees, of which the *Riji* are customarily vice chairmen, and which plan and execute party strategy in the Diet (Baerwald 1974:84). The House Management Committee, the *Riji*, and the chairmen and other vice chairmen of the parties' Diet Policy Committees constitute the core of the *kokutaizoku* ("Diet strategy types"), who with the speaker provide the nearest thing to a specialized "Parliamentary leadership" in the Japanese system.

In the 1950s and 1960s these legislative "conflict managers" were not in a position to really "lead." For example, the speaker, since 1955 always a senior

LDP politician, was ultimately subject to the orders of the prime minister who used him to force snap votes and then, in a ritualistic gesture to appease the boycotting opposition parties into resuming normal business, had him take responsibility for the incident and resign. Between 1947 and 1973, the speaker's average term in office was exceedingly short (twenty months) with most resigning following a confrontation incident (Kishimoto 1977: 177, 180). Within the LDP the speakership was often treated like any other Cabinet post, doled out to an aging legislator according to criteria of long party service and factional balance (Kishimoto 1977:181). The snap-vote routine led opposition parties to view the speaker not as the institution's even-handed leader but as the representative of LDP partisan interests.

The "Diet strategy types" (*kokutaizoku*) on the House Management Committee and in the parties' Diet Policy Committees also had little power, compared to "policy types" (*seichōzoku*). Legislation was formulated in the bureaucracy, refined and amended in the LDP Policy Affairs Research Council (PARC) and its divisions, and then approved by a cabinet which had an easy majority in the Diet. LDP *kokutaizoku* only implemented the prior decisions of their party's leadership; in the opposition they worked to wrest trivial and largely symbolic concessions from their LDP counterparts. Lacking independent authority within their parties, they were "were not free in their negotiations" but rather were "agents of hostile—on occasion warring—camps" (Baerwald 1974:85).

My interviews in 1978 revealed in two ways the new importance of parliamentary leadership: recent speakers and Diet strategy specialists (a) have career patterns manifesting greater status and political expertise and (b) are developing greater independence and authority vis-a-vis political party leaders.

(a) Between 1973 and 1979 there were only two speakers of the lower house, Maeo Shigesaburō and Hori Shigeru. Although they were as usual "grand old men" of the LDP, with at least ten terms of service in the House, Maeo and Hori brought to the position some unusual attributes. Maeo was a former leader of a major faction in the party (the old Ikeda, now Ōhira faction) and erstwhile candidate for the party presidency and prime ministership. Hori had been Prime Minister Satō's close factional and party lieutenant during the latter's long term as prime minister and a power broker between LDP factions after Satō's retirement (Shimizu 1979a). Both had been secretary general of the party.

More importantly, Maeo and Hori when named to the speaker's post still wielded considerable power and influence within the LDP, influence nearly commensurate with that of the prime minister himself. Their being appointed, as a number of my interviewees argued, was symbolic of the speakership's having become more important as legislative relations with the opposition had become a more vital element in governing. Their status in the party also enabled them, as we shall see, to transform the speaker's role.

The career patterns of the "Diet strategy types" on the House Management Committee and the parties' Diet Policy Committees also underwent a change after the advent of the *hakuchū jidai*. In an interview in 1978, the LDP chairman of the House Management Committee told me that the "quality" of the opposition party *Riji* had improved during the 1970s. Opposition-party directors in turn said that during the 1970s the LDP politicians appointed as chairmen had greater cabinet-level experience, and after their incumbency moved again into very responsible high-level posts, indicating that the LDP has come to value the political skills in dealing with the opposition that such service provides. Particularly, they noted that the very sensitive position of director general of the Defense Agency (a ministerial cabinet position) and the chairmanship of the House Management Committee have become linked in recruitment patterns with a number of recent chairmen either coming from that cabinet position or being appointed to it subsequently.

It occurred to me that my interviewees might be perceiving a broader change in LDP political recruitment patterns: namely, that "Diet strategy types" in general might be becoming more important than "policy types" as the skills of legislative conflict management and of bargaining with the opposition parties have become more necessary to the party. To test this hypothesis, I calculated the number of major cabinet, legislative, and party positions held by "Diet strategy types" (chairmen and directors of the House Management Committee and chairmen and vice chairmen of the LDP Diet Policy Committee). For comparison, I performed a similar calculation for the chairmen and vice chairmen of the LDP's PARC and a random sample consisting of one chairman and a number of directors of several policy-oriented committees in the House (using these as the policy equivalent of the House Management Committee directors). Because the *hakuchū* era began in 1976, the calculation was performed for those serving in the above positions as of April, 1973 and as of February, 1978. The results are presented in Table 1.

TABLE 1

"Diet Strategy Types" vs. "Policy Types":
Career Patterns, 1973-74 and 1978-79
(Unit = Positions Held/Number of Individuals)

Backgrounds (Pre-1973 and 1978)	Diet Strategy Types		Policy Types	
	1973 (N=12)	1978 (N=14)	1973 (N=12)	1978 (N=14)
Cabinet-Level Positions	.08	.21	1.00	.35
Sub-Cabinet-Level Positions	1.00	1.56	1.25	.93

TABLE 1 (continued)

	Diet Strategy Types		Policy Types	
House Committee Chairmen	.08	.21	1.41	1.07
Higher Party Executive	.17	.07	.25	.14
Later Careers (By 1974 and 1979)[1]				
Cabinet-Level Positions	.17	.29	.67	.43
Sub-Cabinet-Level Positions	.33	.14	.08	.14
House Committee Chairmen	.08	.28	.17	.07
Higher Party Executive	.25	.14	.17	.07

Sources: Seiji Kōhō Sentā 1973, 1975, 1978, 1980.

1. "Later Careers" indicates positions held after such service until December 1974 or December 1979. The samples are thus comparable across roughly equivalent time periods of twenty and twenty-two months, both encompassing a change of administration (Tanaka to Miki and Fukuda to Ōhira).

The data indicate clearly that in 1973 policy types had much superior career backgrounds to "Diet strategy types" in all categories of elite political positions. As for later careers, service in important party and Diet policy positions was clearly a greater boost to subsequent political career chances than service in important Diet strategy posts (although judging from the fall-off in the ratio of positions at all levels for both types, numerous members of the samples had reached the culmination of their party and Diet careers by 1973).

By 1978, however, the pattern changes. Policy types in this later period bring to their roles less cumulative party and Diet experience than in 1973 in all categories of background positions and fare worse in later appointments than they did in 1973, except at the relatively unimportant subcabinet level of vice minister. By contrast, "Diet strategy types" in 1978 show marked increases in total political background experiences and were appointed to more cabinet-level positions and House committee chairmanships in 1978-79 than they were in 1973-74.

Career patterns in the LDP are undoubtably influenced by many other factors, but these data and the testimony of my interviewees indicate that "Diet strategy types" in the *hakuchū* era were recruited from representatives with greater political expertise and that their tenure in key Diet strategy positions was better rewarded in subsequent appointments because dealing with the opposition parties in the Diet had become more crucial to the LDP. Although a policy orientation remains a major attribute for political leadership in the LDP, and will likely remain so as long as the LDP continues governing, the relative importance of parliamentary leadership appears to have been increasing in the party.

(b) Parliamentary leaders also have developed greater independence and authority. Maeo Shigesaburō, using his prestige and influence within the LDP, began the process of transforming the speakership. Upon taking the post (1973), Maeo gave up his party affiliation to symbolize his commitment to making the position a suprapartisan one. More importantly, during his tenure in office he consistently treated all parties in an even-handed manner and attempted to make the speaker's main function the impartial facilitation of the legislative process. Many of my interviewees credited Maeo with establishing new norms for the speakership and altering its image among the opposition parties.

These new norms have become firmly established. Hori Shigeru had been perceived as a hard-liner in his career as LDP politician, but as speaker he continued Maeo's impartial and suprapartisan management of House affairs. The next speaker, Nadao Hirokichi, was also known as a "hawk" on certain issues within in the LDP, but on assuming the speakership he publicly committed himself to continuing the policies of his predecessors (on Hori and Nadao, see Shimizu 1979a). In my interviews in 1978 I found a nearly universal consensus among parliamentary and party leaders that the speaker's expected role was to be a neutral arbiter of partisan conflict and that his formal decisions, when solicited, are considered binding (for further details, see Krauss, forthcoming). The speaker's autonomy has increased to the point that he will sometimes intervene informally within the LDP to preempt a party action he believes will lead to great conflict or disorder in the Diet. Hori, for example, played a role in convincing Prime Minister Fukuda to compromise with the opposition on the 1977 budget (Shimizu 1979a). Reflecting their increased authority and independence, both Maeo and Hori served terms as speaker far exceeding the postwar average, and both resigned voluntarily, unlike most former speakers who were forced out as the sacrificial victims of LDP snap-vote strategies.

My interviews also elicited evidence that the directors of the House Management Committee have developed somewhat greater authority to negotiate interparty legislative compromises. Still generally bound by the limits of concession set by intraparty discussions, the directors I interviewed in 1978 increasingly saw their role as more than partisan advocates; they also now took seriously their other role as the speaker's advisors, responsible for smooth legislative process. Nowadays, they noted, they frequently negotiate a compromise among themselves and then try to persuade their party's Diet Policy

Committee to accept it. In such cases, they expect, and almost always receive, the backing of that committee's chairman in fulfilling the promises they have made to rival party directors. Such promises are taken seriously by the directors because of the ties of trust and friendship that develop among them.

In sum, there seems to be a trend toward the development of institutional norms in competition with partisan demands among these parliamentary leaders, norms of greater autonomy to negotiate their own binding agreements to settle legislative conflicts and of being more authoritative legislative advocates within the party decision process.

Conclusions

In the 1950s and 1960s, the political environment in Japan introduced extreme partisan and conflictual elements into the Diet's basic "arena" organization. During the last decade, however, changes in voting behavior, the party system, public expectations, and the political climate altered the organizational context and the political role of the Diet. As a result of the new party balance of power and opposition influence in committee management, "transformative" elements became apparent: enhanced ability of the legislature to check the executive, increased importance of committee politics, greater power to modify legislation, and pressures for accommodation of conflicting partisan goals.

With these changes in organizational context, a new parliamentary role culture emerged among political leaders:

(1)   Party leaders were under strong pressure to reconcile intraparty interests with interparty compromise in the Diet.

(2)   Parliamentary leaders had greater political experience and increasingly were being recruited to influential government and party posts.

(3)   Parliamentary leaders (speaker, House Management Committee *Riji*) acquired more autonomy and authority vis-a-vis party leaders.

These trends in leadership roles greatly affected the political process in Japan by the end of the 1970s. First, there was an expansion in the size, scope, and diversity of the real decision-making elite in Japan. The old bureaucracy-LDP-big business triad remained influential coordinators of Japanese economic and public policy;   but to them were added, at a minimum, the top leaders of the opposition parties and their major support groups and the chief parliamentary leaders, who were formerly on the fringes of real influence.

Second, decision making became increasingly complex and arduous, incorporating a larger set of often contradictory demands. Every political leader in Japan encountered dilemmas of intra- vs. interparty demands, of partisan organizational goals vs. parliamentary institutional values, of symbolic affirmation of ideological principle vs. utilitarian compromise, and of the need to conform to public expectations vs. the necessity for retaining maximum room for private maneuver. The potential for shifting coalitions on each issue became greater, and the likelihood of semipermanent, intraelite alliances was lessened.

Third, the site for the resolution of the complex and multisided process of accommodation among competing elites shifted toward the legislative arena where the interests of this more diverse elite met. Legislative government shared the limelight of Japanese politics along with administrative and party government.

It was therefore not accidental that 1979-80 saw the unprecedented selection of a prime minister, Ōhira, on the floor of the Diet, rather than decided by intra-LDP consensus prior to the vote. In this election, Ōhira edged out his party rival, Fukuda, because the opposition parties abstained from voting. Within a few months, Ōhira's government was to fall in a no-confidence vote (the first time an LDP government had ever been so defeated on the floor of the Diet) when the same opposition parties voted against him and the rival factions of his own party failed to support him. In these recent events can be seen the convergence of all the trends I have been discussing: the expanded scope of the influential political elite, the difficulties of attaining and maintaining a wide consensus among the competing interests of a diverse leadership, and the Diet as the new focal point of intra- and interparty conflicts.

A final consequence of the new leadership role expectations was the paradox that the very trends that complicated the tasks of partisan leadership in Japan also created new ways to handle them through the legislative process. The development of parliamentary bargaining skills and of a more experienced, influential parliamentary leadership, such as I have described, was also the basis for new legislative conflict-management mechanisms and rules of the parliamentary game (Krauss, forthcoming). And these, in turn, produced less intense overt conflict and fewer breakdowns in government-opposition communication and relations during the *hakuchū* era than at any other time in postwar history.

The changes I have discussed may not be completely positive for Japanese democracy and political economy (see Krauss, forthcoming). Nor may they be permanent. In the June 22, 1980, election precipitated by the success of the opposition-sponsored, no-confidence resolution that toppled Ōhira, the LDP won an unexpected overwhelming victory at the polls. Capturing over 280 seats in the House of Representatives (as well as a majority of the House of Councillors), the LDP recaptured control over all the important standing committees in the lower house and thus once again over the legislative process. Whether this new development will completely reverse the leadership trends of the last decade, or whether the habits of cross-party communication and of increased priority to legislative affairs survive, become the crucial questions in the early 1980s.

Whatever the future of leadership roles, their transformation during the 1970s provides us with at least one important lesson about the study of leadership in Japan. As I noted at the beginning of this paper, most leadership studies have focussed on the perennial patterns of leadership style. Even during the *hakuchū* era, these "traditional" norms applied: organizational veterans whose preferred *modus operandi* was consensus and decision making in small face-to-face groups were still being recruited to leadership positions. Nevertheless, leadership role expectations were only partly determined by culture; they also changed in response to a changing environment. Influential party veterans were placed in parliamentary leadership positions and not just party or governmental ones; legislative leaders had some autonomy and authority and not just symbolic prestige; consensus had to be sought among rival parties as well as within one's own party; the context of interpersonal decision making had shifted to formal legislative or more public sites. These changes had significant effects on politics in Japan, sometimes exacerbating conflict within parties while contributing to more compromise in government-opposition relations and to making the Diet a more stable and important legislature.

Thus, if "traditional" styles of leadership endure, their meaning and consequences will vary depending on the power relationships and institutional arrangements in which they operate. Cultural styles of leadership do not, in and of themselves, guarantee organizations or institutions that will perform in certain ways. "Traditional" norms can contribute in modern contexts *either* to unity *or* divisiveness, stability *or* instability, harmony *or* conflict. Leadership is a function performed in a changing environment of power and organization. How cultural preferences combine with that environment determines the problems and consequences of leadership.

References

Adachi Toshiaki. 1974. *Kokkai kaizōron* (Views on Diet reform). Tokyo: Nagata Shobō.

Allinson, Gary. 1976. Japan's independent voters: dilemma or opportunity? *The Japan Interpreter* 11:36-55.

Baerwald, Hans H. 1964. Parliament and parliamentarians in Japan. *Pacific Affairs* 37:271-82.

_____. 1970. Nikkan kokkai: the Japan Korea Treaty Diet. In L. W. Pye, ed., *Cases in comparative politics: Asia*. Boston: Little, Brown, and Co.

_____. 1974. *Japan's parliament: an introduction*. London: Cambridge University Press.

Braden, Wythe Edward. 1979. Japanese leadership: a profile. *PHP* 10:27-64.

DiPalma, Giuseppe. 1973. *The study of conflict in western society*. Morristown, New Jersey: General Learning Corporation.

_____. 1977. Parliamentary responses to regime crisis: a problem of institutionalization. Paper prepared for the Seminar on the Italian Crisis, Turin, Italy, March, 1977.

Endicott, John E. 1977. The 1975-76 debate over ratification of the NPT in Japan. *Asian Survey* 17:275-92.

Japan Times Weekly. 1979. Lower house narrowly approves '79 budget. March 17, p. 1.

Kim, Yong C. 1975. The committee system in the Japanese Diet: recruitment, orientation, and behavior. In G. R. Boynton and Chong Lim Kim, eds., *Legislative systems in developing countries*. Durham, North Carolina: Duke University Press.

Kishimoto Kōichi. 1977. Shūsan gichō no isu no nukumori (The hotseat of the House Speakers). *Chūō Kōron* VV:174-83.

Kosaka Masataka. 1969. Kyōkō saiketsu no seijigaku (The politics of the snap vote). *Chūō Kōron* VV:50-69.

Krauss, Ellis S. Forthcoming. Toward the institutionalization of conflict management in Japan's parliament. In T. Rohlen, P. Steinhoff, and E. Krauss, eds., *Conflict in Japan*.

Mainichi Shimbun. 1978. Yūji rippō: kōmei ga itten 'hantai' (The emergency mobilization bill: the Clean Government Party's about-face to opposition). September 7, p. 2.

Mainichi Shimbunsha, eds. 1977. *Seikyoku-rengō jidai* (The political situation: the age of coalition). Tokyo: Mainichi Shimbunsha.

Nakane Chie. 1970. *Japanese society*. Berkeley: University of California Press.

Packard, George R. 1966. *Protest in Tokyo: the security treaty crisis of 1960*. Princeton: Princeton University Press.

Pempel, T. J. 1975. The dilemma of parliamentary opposition in Japan. *Polity* 8:63-79.

Polsby, Nelson. 1975. Legislatures. In F. Greenstein and N. Polsby, eds., *Handbook of political science*. Reading, Massachusetts: Addison-Wesley.

Scalapino, Robert A., and Junnosuke Masumi. 1962. *Parties and politics in contemporary Japan*. Berkeley: University of California Press.

Seiji Handobukku (Handbook of politics) 1973, 1975, 1978, 1979, 1980. Tokyo: Seiji Kōhō Sentā.

Shimizu Minoru. 1979a. The new and former House Speakers. *Japan Times Weekly*. February 17, p. 4.

_____. 1979b. Nishioka resigns: will NLC disintegrate? *Japan Times Weekly*, July 28, p. 4.

_____. 1979c. Ōhira, pretty tough politician. *Japan Times Weekly*, November 24, p. 4.

Steiner, Kurt, Ellis Krauss, and Scott Flanagan, eds. 1980. *Political opposition and local politics in Japan*. Princeton: Princeton University Press.

Thayer, Nathaniel B. 1976. The mathematics of an effective majority in the Japanese Diet. Revised version of an unpublished paper, School of Advanced International Studies, Johns Hopkins University.

MAYORAL LEADERSHIP IN JAPAN:
WHAT'S IN A SEWER PIPE?

Ronald Aqua

Cultural and public facilities may be built and prosperous business streets developed above the ground, but a city without a completed sewerage system is no more than a slum.

—Suzuki Heizaburō, former mayor of Mitaka city; from his *Chōsen 20-nen: waga shisei* (Twenty years of challenge: our municipal government), 1975:20.

Directly in front of the imposing and modernistic Mitaka city hall in suburban Tokyo stands a unique—almost bizarre—public monument, one that would seem more likely to provoke quiet laughter than thoughtful reverence. It is a section of a meter-high concrete sewer pipe, boldly inscribed with the following message:

Public Sewerage 100% Completed
Next: 100% Flush Toilets
We are Building a City With an Excellent Environment
and Excellent Social Welfare

To all but the most recent inhabitants of this rapidly growing bedroom suburb, the monument and its inscription are readily identified with Suzuki Heizaburō, Mitaka's highly esteemed "doctor-mayor." The bluntness and pragmatism suggested by the monument embody Suzuki's style of leadership during an eventful twenty-year administration, and to ask how that particular sewer pipe came to be erected *above* the ground is to ask about the life of this strong-willed and tough-minded politician.

This article will consider Mayor Suzuki's career in the broader framework of mayoral leadership in postwar Japan. The Mitaka case is only one of many that might have been selected for analysis, but the appeal of this particular one lies in the very longevity of the Suzuki regime and its prominence on the national political scene. Close observation of the Mitaka case offers a unique opportunity to monitor the changing course of central-local relations during the postwar period. It also provides rare glimpses into the innermost workings of that intricate web of public affairs known as "intergovernmental relations." But most importantly for my purposes, it affords the chance to observe first-hand those leadership qualities which are required of local chief executives as they grapple with the complex issues involved in governing an advanced technological society.

In Japan, as elsewhere, it seems reasonable to expect that leadership styles and roles will vary both among different levels of government (i.e., central vs. local) and across units at the same level (i.e., cities or central ministries). Such variation reflects different (or changing) organizational contexts (see Krauss, in this volume) as well as personal differences that individuals bring with them to office. Despite the possible significance of these differences in role and style for the overall functioning of the political system, researchers have tended to overlook the leadership factor in their attempts to analyze such phenomena as changes in electoral trends, shifts in policy orientation, and alterations in power-brokerage relationships among major competing interests on the national scene. Rather, "leadership" as a departure for analysis has often been relegated in importance or subsumed in that amorphous generality "culture."

The present study documents a case of particularly dynamic local leadership and examines in some detail how such leadership can make a difference in the conduct of local affairs. The case at hand is colorful and suggestive, but no argument will be made for its applicability to local governments more generally. Still, it should prove useful in setting the stage for a discussion of recruitment patterns and leadership styles at the local level. And this, in turn, will lead to some concluding remarks about the role of local leadership within the national political system.

Suzuki's Life and Times

Suzuki Heizaburō was born in Mitaka in 1906 when it was still a placid farming village of 5,000 inhabitants, close to the center of Tokyo but largely untouched by the vast social changes then taking place. Suzuki's family had deep roots in the region, extending back more than 300 years. He attended primary school in Mitaka and thereafter enrolled in a more cosmopolitan middle school in the Shinjuku area of Tokyo. As a young man, he entered a school of foreign languages and dreamt of one day traveling to South America, but his plans were cut short by his grandfather, who, having studied medicine in a Dutch-run academy in Nagasaki, insisted that Heizaburō pursue a similar course. The young Suzuki thereupon found himself "imprisoned" in the medical department of Nihon University, where he continued his study of foreign language with more determination than he could muster for medicine. He became particularly interested in German and by chance had contact with an instructor who had just returned from Germany with a copy of Marx's *Das Kapital*, which Suzuki studied not so much for its substance as for the practice in German. In time, however, Suzuki came to feel that his prolonged contact with Marxist writings exerted a strong influence on his thinking about politics and society.

Suzuki finished his medical studies and in August of 1933 opened a small maternity clinic in front of the Mitaka railroad station. Not long thereafter, in March 1937, he ran successfully for election to the Mitaka village assembly and at the same time became involved in the activities of the Japan Socialist Party under the tutelage of Dietman Nakamura Takaichi. (Nakamura, a Dietman from Tokyo, became known in the postwar years as a member of the JSP's right wing.) Suzuki's medical practice and political career were interrupted by military service as a noncombatant medical officer in China, where he remained from October 1940 to the time of his repatriation in April 1946. He found his military experience to be an excellent opportunity not only to improve his medical skills, but also to engage in various administrative, financial, educational, and public health pursuits.

At the war's end Suzuki returned to Mitaka where he immediately became involved in the revitalized JSP. He served as district chairman of the party and, for a brief period, was the chairman of Mitaka's public safety commission. In the early 1950s Suzuki was employed as a lecturer and research associate in the department of public health at Nihon University's medical school, and while there he conducted a study of the relationship between poverty, the living environment, human development, and disease. The major finding of his study, which culminated in a doctoral thesis in 1954, was that human longevity was closely correlated with the quality of the environment (particularly adequate sanitation and housing).

Suzuki had little difficulty integrating his academic training with his socialist politics. He eventually decided to translate his public health background and his strong social consciousness into political action. He felt the need to take a personal hand in creating a healthy environment for his own community and thus announced his candidacy for mayor of Mitaka in 1955. His overriding policy objective had already crystalized: to undertake projects that would respect human life and assure equal access for all citizens to a long and healthy existence.

Suzuki was elected mayor and assumed office under less than favorable circumstances. The city was in debt and lacked even the most basic urban amenities, despite a growing population that had already passed 75,000. There was no water or sewerage system. The schools were wooden firetraps, and the city hall was a "patchwork of creaking wood." Most city "streets" were no more than rutted dirt lanes that were mudtraps during rainy weather and dustbins during dry weather.

Suzuki built a community water system, and then established three
priorities that were to remain his policy objectives for the duration of his
administration:

(1) the completion of a municipal sewerage network which would
    provide service to all local residents;
(2) the replacement of unsound and unsafe educational buildings with
    modern and fireproof facilities; and
(3) the establishment of a social welfare program which would assure
    the maintenance of high health standards after a basic
    infrastructure (i.e., the sewer system) was in place.

The last point evolved into a community development program whose origins could
be traced to similar programs Suzuki observed in West Germany.

According to Suzuki, the completion of a sewerage project was a sine qua
non for the success of the other programs. He frequently wrote in the city's
official newsletter lamenting the lack of "sewer consciousness" among the
Japanese people, despite the fact that sewer systems had long histories in the
advanced Western nations. He noted that until recently Japanese farmers relied
heavily on human excrement as a source of fertilizer and that the many streams
and rivers in Japan's mountainous regions seemed to preclude the need for
extensive underground drainage networks. But changing agricultural practices and
alterations in the landscape brought about by industrialization required
adjustments in these outmoded notions. Suzuki bemoaned the fact that even in
recent times public officials seemed to prefer conspicuous above-ground
construction projects over the installation of sewer pipes that could not be seen by
local residents. Local governments avoided sewerage projects, seeking other, less
expensive methods of maintaining minimum sanitary conditions (such as the
widespread use of inoculations to control typhoid, cholera, and other water-borne
diseases). For these reasons, international comparisons of sewerage networks
placed Japan among the least advanced of the industrialized countries.

Mitaka city received approval from the Ministry of Construction for its
sewerage plans in 1958 and a year later embarked on an ambitious ten-year
construction program. City officials were to find that higher-level support for the
project was less than enthusiastic, however, as prefectural and central officials
busied themselves with public works projects geared to rapid industrialization. Six
years after the project had begun, it was seriously impeded by a shortage of funds
despite the fact that only 25 percent of the contruction had been completed.
Suzuki was advised by Ministry of Construction officials to circumvent the cash-
flow problem by introducing a "user's fee" for houses already hooked up to city
sewer lines. This was permitted by national law and by 1965 had already been
adopted by forty cities. When Suzuki proposed the user's fee to the city assembly,
however, it was opposed by Socialist assemblymen on orders from party

headquarters. He later recounted that he felt the local Socialists knew they were voting against the city's best interests, but that there was little they could do other than to obey their party's instructions. This incident was to have a lasting influence on Suzuki's own relationship with the JSP and on his perceptions of the party's role in local affairs. He later stated that while he endorsed the main body of socialist doctrine, as a mayor of a city he had to act in the best interest of all the residents even when partisan interests demanded otherwise. Although Suzuki is usually considered "progressive" because of his forward-looking programs and his socialist ties, he took steps in the later years of his administration to separate himself both from the Socialists and from the National Association of Progressive Mayors.

The user's fee was eventually implemented over the objections of Socialist assemblymen, but Mitaka officials found that even this additional revenue source failed to cover many of the expenses connected with the sewerage project. Suzuki thereupon intensified his lobbying efforts with the prefectural and central governments, and also introduced several reforms aimed at rationalizing the local bureaucracy, hoping thereby to channel any surplus funds to the sewerage project. Among the major retrenchment measures taken were:

(1) careful control over the number of new administrative positions created;
(2) delegation of authority downward so as to decrease the number of time-consuming bureaucratic delays;
(3) entrusting certain municipal functions to the private sector (most notably trash collection); and
(4) establishing training programs for city officials to familiarize them with the principles of industrial management and "higher productivity with fewer workers."

Training included study trips to other countries, a privilege clearly perceived as a strong inducement to greater efficiency and one ordinarily reserved for promising officials in central government agencies.

Through these and other measures Suzuki was ultimately able to acquire the money needed to complete his prized sewerage project. He also left the city in better financial condition than he had found it. A 5 percent spending deficit at the time he took office had been transformed into a 5 percent surplus by the time he retired in 1975—and this despite the staggering costs of the sewerage project, which at the height of construction reached one quarter of the city's outlays for the fiscal year (1970). More was involved in this improved financial picture, however, than Suzuki's policies alone account for. Changing public attitudes toward the environment and social welfare made central and prefectural agencies show greater interest in programs such as sewer construction, especially after 1969. In fact, the central government's share of financing for sewerage construction had increased from 13.5 percent in 1959 (when Suzuki launched his program) to 24.5 percent by 1972 (a year before the Mitaka project was completed; figures from Japan Ministry of Construction, *Nihon no gesuido—sono genjō to kadai* (Japan's sewerage—present conditions and prospects), 1974:70-71). By that time many other cities had also embarked upon ambitious sewerage programs.

On October 17, 1973, Suzuki's dream of making Mitaka the first city in Japan to have a complete sewerage system was fulfilled. The city had also made impressive strides toward fulfilling Suzuki's goal of upgrading the local educational plant. Only the third of Suzuki's goals, the provision of high-quality social welfare services, remained. Suzuki hoped to construct a multi-functional "community center," based on designs he had seen during a tour of West German municipalities. Plans for the center grew out of Suzuki's conviction that rapid socioeconomic and demographic changes had eroded traditional bases of communalism, and that the city government should do everything in its power to revitalize community pride and civic spirit. Suzuki envisioned the "community program" as a logical extension of his sewerage project. The completed sewerage system was to be the first step toward a better living environment, just as the implementation of a "community plan" would be the first step toward a better social environment.

Suzuki ended his tenure as mayor in 1975, declaring to his supporters that his major goals had been achieved and that there seemed to be little else he could do for the community. He qualified the latter remark by noting that factionalism and partisanship had become increasing burdens on his administration and that the time had come for a new leadership to assert itself. He would thus return to his private medical practice and continue his lifelong efforts to improve the health of others.

An Assessment

Suzuki Heizaburō's career offers a richly textured montage of the various elements that shape and define local politics and policy making. Here I would like to comment on those aspects of Suzuki's administration that bear upon local priority setting, conflict resolution, and the provision of essential municipal services, as well as his personal interaction with various political and administrative figures.

Priority Setting

Suzuki's policy objectives derived from his medical background and his social convictions. He plunged Mitaka city headlong into a costly sewerage project at a time when the need for such projects was barely recognized as legitimate by the central or prefectural governments. In deciding that Mitaka would have sewerage service for all its residents, he did not comply with national standards.   Rather, he followed his own professional judgment as a medical practitioner and public servant.   His medical and administrative ties served him well in his unrelenting efforts to have his proposals accepted by officials in key central agencies.   Medical colleagues in the Ministry of Health and Welfare, for example, could scarcely deny the relationship between high-quality sewerage service and human longevity, especially when Suzuki supported his argument with statistical analyses that he himself had prepared.

Although Suzuki had associated himself with the JSP, he managed to estab-lish channels of communication with mainstream Liberal Democratic Party politicians. In fact, he flatly advised socialists to be prepared to work within the confines of a capitalist economy.   As mayor, and as chief spokesman on policy matters for all the residents of his city, he shunned party labels and preferred instead to run as an "independent" in local elections. His bitter criticisms of the local Socialist assemblymen who voted against his proposal for the user's fee further served to set him at a distance from JSP activities.

Suzuki also knew his constituency well and had a keen sense of the limit to which local residents could be taxed to finance his programs. He was a seasoned politician whose electoral career dated from the prewar days.   His support base was not highly susceptible to partisan or other organized pressures. Thus, he was in a position, politically speaking, to set local priorities which he felt best served his city's interests, however much out of step he may have been with the central government's program of industrialization and rapid economic growth.

If Suzuki's forceful style seems uncharacteristic of Japanese leadership, his effectiveness in establishing priorities for his city is not at all untypical for a city mayor, according to a survey I conducted among more than 350 higher-ranking bureaucrats in thirty-seven medium-sized municipalities throughout Japan.   In that survey, I first asked the respondents to state which programs had received highest priority in their cities. I then asked them to indicate whom they saw as the prime force behind those priorities.   A majority of the respondents, 59.3 percent, indicated that the priorities reflected the mayor's own programs. Only 29.3 percent felt the priorities reflected the interests of "ordinary citizens." When asked whether these priorities were based on local, as opposed to prefectural or central government, initiatives, 82.7 percent responded that the priorities were strictly local in origin, thus strengthening the conclusion that the mayor's role was a crucial one in determining the course of local governmental policy.

Conflict Resolution

Very early in his administration, Suzuki realized his expensive sewerage project required developing a "sewer consciousness" among local residents, so they could see where and how their money would be spent. Suzuki thus embarked on an intensive campaign of education involving the skillful use of the city's public information organs and numerous public meetings with residents. These efforts bore fruit in the lack of significant organized opposition to the project. So successful was the public relations campaign, in fact, that many residents looked with pride to the prospect of their city's becoming the first in Japan to have complete sewerage service. Good timing also helped—much of the project had been completed by the time the new obstructionist "citizens' movements" began to appear in Mitaka and elsewhere.

Suzuki used similar tactics in bargaining with the central government officials who would be asked to provide an increasing share of funding for the project. Rather than risk antagonizing these officials by lecturing them on socialist doctrine or by criticizing high growth policies, Suzuki went on the offensive with practical arguments bolstered by flawless documentation. He appealed to nationalistic pride by pointing to Japan's embarrassingly low standing among the industrial countries in its "sewerage rating." And he demanded that politicians act on their own stated commitment to enhance the general welfare of the Japanese people.

Suzuki's uneasy relationship with the JSP tested his conflict-solving abilities to the limit. But he knew that after he had achieved some initial policy successes, he would become more valuable to the Socialists than they were to him. Thus, he could speak with impunity of the need to disregard directives from party headquarters (i.e., in the "user's fee" dispute) when those directives blocked his own policies, knowing that he could still count on a JSP endorsement at the next election. This situation bespoke the Socialists' weak organization at the grass-roots level and their need to rely on support groups sustained by and for particular local strongmen.

Provision of Services

Suzuki sometimes compared his city's performance in delivering essential municipal services to the performance of nearby cities—but more often than not, his comparisons were international in scope. He frequently traveled to observe conditions in other countries and was particularly fond of pointing out that at a point when the financial shortfall of the sewerage project was greatest, he received inspiration to continue his struggle by attending an international symposium on the environment in Seattle in 1963. He also liked to point out that his "community project" was not a carbon copy of "community" plans being propagated by the Ministry of Home Affairs, but one based on "international" models.

Suzuki insisted that criteria for efficiency set by the private sector could be applied to municipal administration, and he personally became involved in many small details of administration to guard against complacency among his staff. As a doctor, for example, he decreed that smoking would be prohibited in all public areas of city hall except for a designated "smoking room." This innovation predated even the recent American preoccupation with "no smoking" rules and was enforced under Suzuki's own watchful eyes. It was a remarkable first in a country where cigarette smoking is quite common even on crowded subways.

Suzuki skillfully used "carrot-and-stick" devices to assure bureaucratic responsiveness. He promised no large salary increases or larger departments, but offered instead greater discretion in decision making to section chiefs, as well as the chance to participate in overseas "study tours." He devoted much effort to having his administrators break with their traditional posture of indifference and arrogance toward the citizens they were supposed to be serving, and at the same time took pains to commend their accomplishments in a conspicuous manner.

The Larger Picture

The policy-making role assumed by Mayor Suzuki fits the general pattern of strong mayoral leadership observed among most of the cities in the sample I surveyed. While it could be argued that mayors in other cities were also unique in terms of their political backgrounds, some biographical data on the mayors in those cities do make it possible to state more general observations about the types of people who become mayor and how they manage their local political environment.

Many of the sampled mayors, like Suzuki, were highly educated people with strong local roots. Only two of them had less than a high-school education, and almost two-thirds had attended a college, university, or professional school beyond the secondary level. All but a few mayors were born in the region where they now lived, and most were born in the cities they now governed.

Some of the mayors in the sample had professional backgrounds similar to Suzuki's—they had been lawyers, doctors, teachers, or union officials prior to running for public office. Several others owned their own businesses or worked for corporations. But fully half of the mayors rose through the ranks of the city or prefectural bureaucracy. Many of them served as deputy mayor (an appointed position) before deciding to run for mayor, either as the incumbent's designated successor or as a challenger to the incumbent.

Suzuki entered public life while in his fifties, and this was not untypical of the sample as a whole. The age of the mayors at the time of their first election ranged from a low of forty-five to a high of seventy-seven. The median age was about fifty-five. For almost half the sample, the mayoral post was the first elected position. The remainder had usually served in the city or prefectural assembly, with the latter more likely. In no case had a mayor been prefectural governor, and only two had served as national Dietmen.

Most of the mayors had, like Suzuki, been loosely associated with a particular political party. There were sixteen "progressives" and twenty-one "conservatives" in the sample. No great distinctions can be drawn between these two groups in terms of their occupational background or political history, but certain differences do surface. A smaller proportion of the progressives had civil service backgrounds, for example, and they also tended to have higher levels of education.

One general impression that emerged from an examination of these data was that mayors of medium-sized Japanese cities are a fairly homogeneous group, especially considering the wide range of city "types" (i.e., industrial, bedtown, regional administrative center, etc.) that were represented in the sample. But the political ideologies of particular mayors might affect the attitudes of their administration's top-ranking civil servants; the final question I wish to address will use some findings from my survey of local civil servants to explore this possibility.

In the survey, I asked the respondents to indicate their own political preference on the conservative-to-progressive spectrum. I then tabulated these responses according to the political ideology of the incumbent mayor and cross-tabulated the same responses with the question in the survey asking who had the greatest influence in setting local priorities.

The first tabulation revealed that a clear majority of bureaucrats serving under conservative mayors identified themselves as conservatives; the same held true for progressives, although the relationship was not as strong. Those who identified themselves as "middle-of-the-road" were evenly distributed across the two mayoral types.

The second tabulation could be regarded as a test of ideological consistency. One might predict that conservative bureaucrats would be more responsive to mayoral priorities than to those articulated by "ordinary citizens," if only because this is assumed to be the traditional posture of civil servants, and conservatives are presumed to be more traditional in their approach to local administration than progressives. By the same logic, progressives might be expected to pay greater attention to citizens' views, since this posture reflects the "progressive" notion of giving a greater voice to the "people."

These expectations were generally borne out. Among conservative bureaucrats, the percentage who regarded the mayor as the most important source of local policy advocacy was greater than the mean for the group as a whole. Progressives, on the other hand, were more inclined to see an important policy-making role for citizens. It is important to remember that a majority of *all* respondents regarded the mayor as the key policy innovator. Still, these cross-tabulations reveal some consistency between ideological preferences and attitudes toward the importance of citizen participation in shaping local policy agendas.

Concluding Remarks

The structural context for local politics in Japan is vastly different than that of the national political arena. Mayors must stand for election on a city-wide basis, rather than in small parliamentary districts, and they must compete for support across diverse constituencies and interests. Once elected, they are given "presidential" powers; their effectiveness in managing their governments does not depend on fragile parliamentary majorities (although they can and do incur policy setbacks by failing to negotiate successfully with the various interests represented in local assemblies). They are, or at least have the potential to be, singularly powerful actors in a political system otherwise dominated by factional leaders who are merely "first among many."

But structure alone cannot account for the very real political influence that local chief executives are able to exert—there is, after all, considerable variation in the extent to which local notables gain prominence at the national level in a system marked by a relatively uniform legal and administrative structure. What has been suggested here is that a major factor contributing to such variation is the style and substance of local executive leadership. In the case of Mitaka, mayoral leadership was informed, aggressive, and highly visible. In the other cases examined as well, it was experienced, mature, and of a quality that commanded loyalty from high-ranking local officials.

The fact that Japanese mayors are successful policy makers is not necessarily surprising or unexpected. What *could* be regarded as surprising is the extent to which these individuals have risen to power in a "political culture" generally thought to be characterized by a colorless, uncharismatic, and bureaucratically oriented leadership at the national level.

Is there, then, more than one "political culture" in Japan? While this brief examination does not pretend to answer that larger question, it does provide evidence that any consideration of political leadership must look at what has been happening below the national level. Only then will it be possible to draw a more complete picture of Japan's present-day political realities.

APPENDIX
Thirty-seven Medium-sized Cities
Comprising the Sample Analyzed

Hakodate	Niigata	Yao
Otaru	Kanazawa	Higashiosaka
Asahikawa	Fukui	Kurashiki
Muroran	Kofu	Kure
Aomori	Nagano	Shimonoseki
Hachinohe	Shizuoka	Tokushima
Sendai	Numazu	Takamatsu
Hitachi	Shimizu	Omuta
Kawaguchi	Yokkaichi	Kurume
Funabashi	Toyonaka	Kumamoto
Matsudo	Suita	Oita
Kamakura	Moriguchi	
Odawara	Hirakata	

POWER BEHIND THE THRONE

Richard J. Samuels

The central relationship in the study of leadership is that between power and authority:

> The leader exercises power, and that he does so accords with the identifications, demands, and expectations of the group. Where the latter are present but little effective power is exercised, we speak of formalistic authority and not leadership. In the converse case, where effective power has not been formalized by the perspectives of authority, we speak of bosses. (Lasswell and Kaplan 1950:152)

Questions of power and authority, of leader and boss, are as old as politics—and as unresolved as ever. But although unresolved, in most polities the tension between the legitimate and the illegitimate exercise of power is widely recognized and frequently addressed in political study (Scott 1972; Caro 1974; Tarrow 1977). In Japanese studies this relationship is intriguing less for its lack of resolution than for its lack of acknowledgement. Only in historical accounts are the powers behind the throne examined in detail; they are largely ignored in contemporary ones (Hurst 1976).

Instead, a different sort of leadership role is stressed. We hear most about the leader as effective manager. Although never synthesized in a single coherent piece of research, there is an uncharacteristic consensus among Japan scholars on the subject of political leadership. Whether the emphasis is placed upon the prominent absence of charismatic leadership (Reischauer 1977), upon personal, as opposed to institutional, sources of authority (Thayer 1969), or upon the abilities

The author gratefully acknowledges the financial assistance provided by State Department and H.E.W. Fulbright awards as well as by the Japan Foundation during 1977–1979, when field research for this essay and for the larger study of which it is a part was conducted. Thanks also are due Sheldon Garon, Terry MacDougall, and Akihiko Tanaka for their helpful comments on an earlier draft of this essay.

of the leader to understand and guide complex patterns of interpersonal relations (Ike 1978), there is a near unanimity among Western observers that leadership in Japanese politics is directed away from open conflict and towards cooperation. This emphasis on leadership as conflict resolution is tied in most analyses to consensual patterns of decision making and to the peculiar dynamics of Japanese group behavior. Nakane's (1970) seminal analysis continues to shape this view of the Japanese leader as one who is able to motivate the group to achieve its objectives by caring for each member in a personal way and by effectively managing interpersonal relations. Thus, Nakane and those who derive their models from her (Yoshino 1968; Ike 1978; Braden 1979) depict a Japanese leader who, if not quite inspiring, is neither always conspiring.

The conspiratorial Japanese political boss does, of course, live in more than the history books, even if social science has failed to systematically explore his many functions. While Nakane is quite correct in pointing out the lack of indigenous terms in Japanese which express the notion of leadership apart from a group context (1970:69), the Japanese have done quite well with a variety of borrowed terms (*riidaa, goddofaazaa, don, bosu, fikusaa,* etc.) all of which correspond to existing, widely recognized leadership roles.[1] There are, moreover, several thoroughly Japanese terms which are applied metaphorically to the more secretive aspects of Japanese political life with which this essay is most concerned. Some, such as *insei,* the retired emperor, and *ōgosho,* the retired shogun, are historically derived and have been applied to the relationship between Tanaka Kakuei and Ōhira Masayoshi, for example.

Political life is everywhere peopled both by those bathed in the spotlight and by those who often exert greater influence from backstage. In the Japanese context, this metaphor is not an idle one; neither is it imposed from abroad. The Japanese use an image from the kabuki theater to suggest the distinction noted above between power and authority. The Japanese political boss is often generically referred to as the *kuromaku* (literally, black veil), the man who sets the stage and assists the actors in full view of all, but who is not supposed to be seen because he is draped in black. Of course, he *is* seen. But like the political boss, he is seen but seldom acknowledged.

It has long been recognized that one secret to political (or any other organizational) success in Japan is an organization's ability to avoid sudden, dramatic confrontations. That ability is best served by the talents of an individual with wide contacts and certain power who can effectively operate apart from the din of press and public in securing agreement (or at least understanding) from all concerned parties before an important action is taken. This highly time-consuming but equally conflict-reducing process of prior consultation is known as

1. They also correspond to the English: leader, godfather, don, boss, and fixer.

nemawashi (literally, binding the roots). It is one of the *kuromaku*'s most sensitive and important functions. He is often responsible for accommodating important persons and groups affected by his policy choices. Thus, the Japanese political boss is not exclusively concerned with clandestine and evil machinations. Even so, he is much more the generalissimo than the lieutenant; his real power ought not be understated. He answers to no one, and his will (if not his vision) is seldom denied. His is a frequently determinant, even if infrequently acknowledged, leadership role.

This essay will compare and contrast two such figures. Neither Matsunaga Yasuzaemon nor Komori Takeshi is typically mentioned as the most prominent political boss in Japan. That designation is usually assigned to others such as Sasagawa Ryōichi or Kodama Yoshio. Nevertheless, Matsunaga, the mainstream conservative, and Komori, the Marxist of uncommon power, had been uniquely (although indirectly) pitted against each other. Each found himself guiding the policy decisions of a handpicked Tokyo Bay Area governor. Each was responsible for the shaping (and the reshaping) of Bay Area development plans at a time of rapid economic growth and unprecedented investment opportunities.[2] Since they were of different ideological bent, a comparison of their respective activities and *modi operandi* affords us the opportunity to analyze the political boss apart from partisan considerations. Let me caution the reader at the outset that I am not arguing that all political decisions (or that all important ones) in Japan are made in smoke-filled teahouses by manipulative and antidemocratic "fixers." This essay is about some which are, but it is more concerned with the process by which those decisions, first conceived as visions of powerful bosses, are transmitted through the offices of authoritative public officials to become implemented as public policy. There is much that is peculiarly Japanese about this process; there is much more that is not. One purpose of this essay is to alert the reader to the difference. A second is to detail an as yet unexplored aspect of political leadership in Japan—power exercised behind the throne.

In comparison to Komori, Matsunaga was by far the more public figure. Born in December, 1875, he is considered the "godfather" of Japan's electric power industry for his role in guiding the postwar redevelopment of the industry. After graduating from Keio Gijuku (later Keio University) in 1896, Matsunaga entered the prestigious Mitsui Bank, which he soon left in order to return to his native Kyushu and a position with the Kyushu Electric Railway Corporation. He subsequently moved to the electric power industry, first in Kyushu, later in Nagoya, and finally in Tokyo, where he arrived in 1928 as the new president of Tōhō Electric. At that time there were five major power companies competing in the Tokyo market, and nine nationwide. As the exigencies of war abroad fed

2. For more detail on the complexity that was the power of each and on the political environment in which each operated, see Samuels 1982.

authoritarianism at home, the government introduced a plan in 1938 to bring together all the major power companies in a single supply network, seeking to eliminate inefficient competition through the creation of this Nihon Hassōden K.K. Matsunaga was among those younger, top-level officials who balked at the forced consolidation order and who resigned their positions. Whether antimilitary, antibureaucratic, a liberal, or a free marketeer—we are left with little more than these descriptions by his associates—Matsunaga was one of the rare members of the economic elite who "sat out" the war. In the end, this was the key to his enormous postwar political power. After many of those who had stayed on to manage the Nihon Hassōden K.K. had been purged by Occupation authorities, Matsunaga was called out of retirement by SCAP to rebuild Japan's decimated power industry. In 1950, he was appointed vice chairman of the newly formed and powerful Public Utilities Commission (Kōeki Jigyō Iinkai), the body designated to rebuild all public utilities nationwide.[3]

Matsunaga's initiative, through the Public Utilities Commission, led to the formation of the immensely influential Electric Power Central Research Institute (Denryoku Chūō Kenkyūjo). The central government had mandated in 1951 that three-thousandths of all electric company profits be allocated to research and development of new power sources. Of that amount, two-thirds was set aside for the creation and sustenance of Matsunaga's Central Research Institute. Formally established in 1951, the Institute began its operations in 1955 with Matsunaga at its helm. His organization's two-thousandths share of the nation's electric power companies' profits quite predictably became a source of Matsunaga's own influence in government. The Central Institute almost immediately emerged as one of the most influential lobbies in Tokyo. Indeed, the Institute was built less as a think tank and planning bureau (although it clearly performed these functions quite professionally) than as a political tool for electric power interests in general, and for Matsunaga's grand development schemes in particular.

His grand schemes were not, however, restricted to electric power generation. Under his direction, the Institute decided to create a separate research body to study non-energy-related development problems. The new Industrial Planning Conference (Sangyō Keikaku Kaigi) was limited only by Matsunaga's vast energy and resources. By the late 1950s it had produced more

---

3. For details on the role of this body, see Otani Ken (1978) and Johnson (1979); details concerning Matsunaga are based upon interviews with Yoda Susumu of the Tokyo Electric Power Company (March 24, 1979), former Chiba Governor Tomono Taketo (February 25, 1979), Itō Mitsuo, former secretariat chief of the Tokyo Bay General Development Council (September 14, 1978), and Ebata Masaki, former Tokyo Metropolitan Port and Harbor Bureau chief engineer and former Matsunaga braintruster (September 25, 1978). Details of Matsunaga's role vis-a-vis the LDP are based upon interviews with a party official who requested anonymity (December 8, 1978, and January 23, 1979).

than two dozen studies, such as Hokkaido development surveys, nationwide water resource plans, and combinat development plans. He engaged the talents of the best young engineers and planners from Tokyo University and industry, and in case after case his aggressive strategy allowed him to take the initiative from the various competing ministries, forcing the government to respond on his terms. At the same time he used his influence to "create demand" for these projects in the localities involved. This two-pronged strategy was not infrequently successful.

The clearest example of this was his role in the development of Tokyo Bay. In July, 1959, the Industrial Planning Conference set forth its "Neo-Tokyo Plan," by far the most comprehensive and influential regional development plan to appear during the high growth era in postwar Japan. In an era of ambitious plans this was a prototype. It called for 400 million square meters of landfill along the Tokyo Bay coasts, and for the creation of an enormous 200 million square meter landfill island directly in the middle of the Bay. In all it proposed that fully two-thirds of Tokyo Bay be filled in. The landfill island in the middle of the Bay was the proposed site of a new central rail and motor transport facility which would connect Tokyo to both the Tohoku and the Chubu regions. Also included were special transport links among the six bay harbor facilities, as were plans for a helioport, a new international jetport, a new heavy industrial belt along the Chiba coast, and two cross-bay bridges. Total landfill costs alone were estimated at ¥4 trillion in 1959 ($11 billion). Matsunaga appointed a former Home Ministry bureaucrat, Kanō Kyūrō, to head the Neo-Tokyo Plan team at its inception in 1956. Kanō, a well-connected expert in land acquisition and finance, subsequently (and not so incidently) became the governor of Chiba in 1962 with the support of the LDP and of Matsunaga.

As noted above, the Matsunaga strategy was two-pronged. He turned first to the Liberal Democratic Party (LDP). At Matsunaga's urging, the LDP created the Tokyo Bay Development Committee within its Policy Affairs Research Council (PARC) in September, 1958. PARC is the highest policy making organ of the LDP and is the umbrella beneath which some seventeen divisions and more than one-hundred committees and councils battle for the party's official endorsement of their programs. Within the party itself initiative was assumed by Prime Minister Kishi Nobusuke, by Policy Affairs Research Council Chief Fukuda Takeo, and by LDP Secretary General Kawashima Shōjirō from Chiba. Fukuda was made the first chairman of the new committee, in spite of the fact that his district is not in the Bay Area. This was important as an effort to broaden the base of support for Tokyo-specific projects within a largely non-Tokyo-based ruling party. It was not sufficient. Initial plans to create a special Tokyo Bay Development Corporation composed of public and private capital, proposed by the committee (again, at Matsunaga's initiative), were killed within the party by those non-Tokyo and antimainstream party leaders (in this case led by Nikaido Susumu) who wanted to see a spatial decentralization of growth, which would directly benefit their own constituencies. Recognizing that there was no clear consensus on making the Tokyo Bay development an LDP priority, Fukuda scrapped the planned corporation.

After being appointed chairman of PARC in January, 1959, Fukuda introduced a second plan, the "Coastal Region Development Law," which would have given developmental priority to all coastal areas, in an attempt to assuage opposition within the party. (Nikaido was from an area in Kyushu which would have been included in this new measure.) It passed smoothly through the party but was stalled three times in the Diet as a result of an unfortunate combination of Cabinet reshuffles, Diet resolutions, and session deadlines. In the midst of these delays, Ikeda, whose support base and priorities were quite different from those of Kishi, formed his first cabinet in July, 1960. He quickly abandoned the coastal regional development scheme and opted instead for his famous "Income Doubling" plan and later for the establishment of regional "New Industrial Cities." It was still very much the high growth game, but the targeted sectors had suddenly been changed. Rather than advocating a plan for spending a great deal in a few coastal areas, a new program of developing new cities in twelve separate regions nationwide was formulated. The Tokyo Bay Development Committee's bill was quietly discarded.[4] The era was one of rapid growth and a conservative's paradise, but it was not always easy for the ruling LDP coalition to agree upon targets of that growth.

Although the national component of Matsunaga's strategy was stalled, Matsunaga was not. Even as the debates were taking place within the LDP and the ministries, he was assembling local support for his ambitious programs. Matsunaga turned at the same time toward the localities in an effort to *create* local demand, to articulate local interests *for* the localities. He developed a "horizontal strategy," bringing together the Bay Area localities into a common organization, which was designed to coordinate local interests and, more importantly, to support the ministries which would articulate those interests at budget time. Acting for and in concert with leading industrial interests and with the help of the LDP, Matsunaga engineered a facade of Bay Area solidarity behind which divergent interests of the region's individual localities could be shielded from view. A coalition of Bay Area localities was created to "cheerlead" the bridge project and other Neo-Tokyo Plan ideas by backing the Construction Ministry's efforts to fund the programs.

4. It should be noted that although the bill originated in the LDP it was submitted to the Diet as a government bill (*seifu teian*). The literature on the Diet suggests that most bills emerge from the bureaucracy, and that there is a clear distinction between those and Dietmen's bills (*giin rippō*). In fact, however, the distinction is fuzzy at best, the choice of form being largely dependent upon political expediency.

The coalitional organization of localities was called the Tokyo Bay General Development Council (Tōkyōwan Sōgō Kaihatsu Kyōgikai, hereafter the Council). It was officially founded in December, 1962, after a characteristically important series of preparatory meetings and agreements among the area's chief industrial and political leaders. In June, 1962, Matsunaga asked Itō Mitsuo, an official of the Yokohama Economic Association and the Kanagawa Chamber of Commerce, to begin this process of bringing together the Bay Area localities and industrial interests into a common organization. Itō's first move was to contact the LDP's Tokyo Bay Development Committee for assistance. The committee's top official, a professional party worker with strong connections in both Chiba and Kanagawa, visited Itō in late June in Yokohama. It was decided at that meeting that the LDP would help Itō and Matsunaga enlist the support of the Bay Area localities; the task of organizing the region's industrial interests for their financial support was left to Matsunaga.

Personal connections with Kanagawa governor Uchiyama and the assurance that there would be no opposition from Chiba, which stood most to gain from integrated industrial development of the Bay, led this LDP official to seek Kanagawa support first. It was Uchiyama who subsequently approached then Tokyo governor Azuma with the plan and who suggested that the chairmanship of the new organization be rotated among the Bay Area's governors instead of being assigned to Matsunaga or another industry spokesman. It was further agreed, however, that the secretariat for the new body be established at Matsunaga's Electric Power Central Research Institute headquarters in downtown Tokyo.

Tokyo needed assurance that the Council was worth creating. It came in the form of LDP intervention with the Finance Ministry in favor of a long-pending Tokyo request for permission to float a ¥3.6 trillion bond issue for improvement of its port facilities. Although the final amount approved was somewhat less than Tokyo had hoped for, the Tokyo Metropolitan government soon became convinced of the power of the Tokyo Bay Development Committee and of the efficacy of membership in the proposed Council.

With the commitment of Tokyo and Kanagawa prefectures secured, and with Chiba anxious for the Council to get under way, the *nemawashi* moved to a more formal plane. On September 12, 1962, a "roundtable research conference" at the New Grand Hotel in Yokohama was hosted by the Kanagawa Economic Research Council.[5] The governors of Tokyo, Chiba, and Kanagawa prefectures, the mayors of dozens of the area's cities, officials of the relevant central ministries, 200 industry leaders, and the press were all in attendance. It was

5. This was one of Matsunaga's local organs. The idea to use Kanagawa people to organize the Council in its early stages was purposefully directed at minimizing the Kawasaki-based opposition to several of the projects.

agreed that a Bay Area council aimed at coordinated, regional development planning was essential. On October 18, a more intimate meeting was held at the headquarters of the Industrial Planning Conference. Attending for Tokyo was then Vice Governor Suzuki Shunichi.[6] The final details concerning the organization and management of the new Council were ironed out, Yokohama and Kawasaki were persuaded to join, and the stage was set for a December inauguration of the body, an inauguration which by no accident was to coincide with the peak of the budget season at the Ministry of Finance.

The Tokyo Bay General Development Council was inaugurated with great hoopla on Christmas Day. Honorary advisors included former Prime Minister Yoshida Shigeru, an old friend of Matsunaga's. The chairmanship was to be rotated annually among the governors of the three member prefectures. An additional 150 directorships were distributed among the other local chief executives and the presidents of private industrial and business firms which were afforded membership. Matsunaga had his Council in place, using it as a forum of support for the original Neo-Tokyo Plan proposals. While outwardly a study group, it was far more active as a pressure group—courting party and government officials, and mobilizing Bay Area officials to cheerlead efforts to fund a number of ambitious plans. Because it depended upon the compliance of local public officials, this component of Matsunaga's strategy could succeed only as long as conservatives continued to dominate local politics in this area.

Conservative political dominance in the Bay Area continued for almost another decade, during which much of the original Neo-Tokyo Plan—the Chiba *combinato*, the bay coast road, the new jetport, etc.—was implemented. But while the struggle continued over some of the more controversial aspects of the Plan, such as the cross-bay bridge between Kawasaki and Kisarazu, local politics were undergoing dramatic changes, particularly in the Tokyo Bay area, as illustrated in Table 1.

TABLE 1
Tokyo Bay Area Chief Executives
During the Life of the
Tokyo Bay General Development Council

TOKYO	Azuma Ryūtarō	(C)	Apr 1959 – Apr 1967
	Minobe Ryōkichi	(P)	Apr 1967 – Apr 1979
	Suzuki Shunichi	(C)	Apr 1979 –

6. Suzuki was elected governor of Tokyo seventeen years later (1979) and almost immediately moved to resurrect several of Matsunaga's still unimplemented plans.

CHIBA	Shibata Hitoshi*	(C)	Dec 1950 - Oct 1962
	Kanō Kyūrō**	(C)	Oct 1962 - Apr 1963
	Tomono Taketo	(C)	Apr 1963 - Apr 1975
	Kawakami Kiichi	(C)	Apr 1975 -
KANAGAWA	Uchiyama Iwatarō	(C)	Apr 1947 - Apr 1967
	Tsuda Bungo	(C)	Apr 1967 - Apr 1975
	Nagasu Kazuji	(P)	Apr 1975 -
SAITAMA	Kurihara Hiroshi	(C)	Jul 1956 - Jul 1972
	Hata Yawara	(P)	Jul 1972 -
KAWASAKI	Kamazashi Fujitarō	(C)	Apr 1947 - Apr 1971
	Itō Saburō	(P)	Apr 1971 -
YOKOHAMA	Nakarai Kiyoshi	(C)	Apr 1959 - Apr 1963
	Asukata Ichio	(P)	Apr 1963 - Apr 1978
	Saigō Michikazu	(C)	Apr 1978 -

*Ran for Diet before end of term.
**Died in office
(C) Conservative   (P) Progressive

When the Council was formed there were LDP-related chief executives in every one of the region's six major localities. By the time the progressive ascendancy had reached its peak in 1975, only Chiba retained a conservative administration. But by then the Council had already been dead for three years, a victim of shifting priorities and the recognition that development meant far more than growth alone. Also gone was the leading figure of that era. Matsunaga Yasuzaemon died in June, 1971, at the age of ninety-five. The Industrial Planning Conference, having been the personal tool of a single man, was effectively dismembered after his death. The industrial elite, of course, was not about to disappear, but never again would it speak as forcefully, as convincingly, and as successfully for Tokyo Bay development as it had under Matsunaga's direction.

The man who killed the Tokyo Bay General Development Council is Matsunaga's foil in this story, Komori Takeshi. He was to the ascendent progressives every bit the power behind the throne that Matsunaga had been to the conservatives who preceded them—and more so. Born in Mashiko in 1912, his career remains very much shrouded in mystery.[7] After graduating from public

7. Much of the account of Komori's life and activities which follows is based upon "The Staff Officer in the Shadow," appropriately appearing as Chapter One of Naitō's (1975) account of the Minobe governorship. The only other published sources are the rather more sensational accounts found in the Japanese weeklies. See Gendai (April 1975); Matsuyama (1978); Honda (1975); Dokusho Shimbun (March 30, 1964); Shūkan Shinchō (June 5, 1971); Shūkan Sankei (March 27, 1975); and Shūkan Sankei (March 10, 1977). The repetition in these articles is great, as

school in that Tochigi village, Komori came to Tokyo to study at the Toshima Normal School, one of the elite public high schools of the prewar period. In his fourth year, just before graduation, he was expelled with twenty others for leading a student strike in protest of conditions in the dormitories and alleged kickbacks by school authorities. He worked first as a private secretary, and later as a journalist with the *Teito Hibi Shimbun* where he made connections which would take him in 1937 to the Shanghai office of the *Tairikiu Shinpō*, a Japanese vernacular daily produced in occupied China with secret army funds. The president of that newspaper, Fuke Shunichi, who asked young Komori to become editor not long thereafter, was to become a key figure in Komori's life. It was Fuke, who in the postwar was to become an LDP Dietman, who also first introduced Komori to Fukuda Takeo, at that time (1941) a Finance Ministry official on loan as advisor to the Nanking government.

This early connection with the future LDP prime minister was to enable Komori to play an extraordinarily flexible role behind the scenes during the Minobe years. Komori's personal connections enabled Minobe to meet Fukuda regularly during their respective tenures as the leading public figures of the two opposing camps (*Asahi Shimbun*, July 14, 1979). Few Japanese leftists could claim such entry into the halls of conservative power. Interestingly, it was also Fuke who introduced Komori to the leftist study group which later became the nucleus of his political power. Fuke first introduced Komori to Takahashi Masao, a leading Marxist economist, who in turn invited Komori to participate in a study group led by himself and Ōuchi Hyōe of Tokyo Imperial University.[8] Although this China-based study group was different from the one which had earlier been rounded up in the 1938 incident, its leadership was largely the same, and it occasionally included also the young Fukuda who had been a student of both Ōuchi and Minobe's father at Tokyo University. This network of associations within which Komori was becoming increasingly intimate, far from being one divided into left and right factions, was essentially one seamless web of elite contacts. Whatever utility there is in partisan labeling must be tempered by a knowledge of the fluidity of these historical associations.

Komori returned to Tokyo in 1944 an established journalist with leftist credentials and conservative contacts. Soon after Japan's defeat, when the lid on

Komori has granted few press interviews in the past decade. For his own statement of his goals for Tokyo, written before Minobe became governor, see Komori (1966).

8. These men were considered dangerously radical by the military government. In an incident closely related to the famous "Popular Front" (*Jinminsensen Jiken*) roundup of 400 leftists in 1937, the members of the so-called "Professors' Group," including Eda Saburō (postwar moderate socialist leader), Minobe Ryōkichi (Tokyo governor 1967-1979), and Ōuchi, were jailed on contrived charges on February 1, 1938. All were bailed out individually by the summer of 1939.

Marxist publications was removed, Komori formed his own publishing company, Kōdosha. This was from the beginning a political operation, a platform for the Takahashi/Ōuchi group's Marxist economics. Komori sponsored a variety of conferences, the work of which he later published; some of these were academic best sellers at the time. It was at this point that he came to know Minobe Ryōkichi, the man whose Tokyo governorship he was not so secretly to share.[9] But the publication of academic best sellers could not prevent the bankruptcy of Kōdosha in 1954, a business failure largely due to Komori's penchant for underwriting the publication of books that pleased him more than his public.

Turning to more partisan instruments, Komori established the Metropolitan Policy Research Institute (Tosei Chōsakai) with Professors Takahashi and Ōuchi in 1955. The financial backing for this left-wing think tank is as unclear as that of the failed publishing house. Although their ties were unquestionably close to organized labor, there is much speculation that a sprinkling of corporate interests, notably Fuji Bank and Tōshiba, were also involved.[10] This institute was ostensibly created as a research organ for the Prefectural Workers' Union and other public labor organizations in Tokyo. Like Matsunaga's Electric Power Central Research Institute, it was more than that. It was established also for the purpose of creating a leftist prefectural government in Tokyo. Its founding coincided with the involvement of Komori and others in the Tokyo gubernatorial campaign of former foreign minister Arita Hachirō who ran in 1955 as a leftist independent against incumbent Yasui Seichirō. Arita had been an old friend from the Kōdosha days, and his candidacy, while not of Komori's making, was the first to receive Komori's support.

The second was four years later when Arita, running as the official Socialist candidate, again failed, this time against popular LDP-backed newcomer Azuma Ryūtarō. Komori's role in the 1959 Arita candidacy earned him the attention of novelist Mishima Yukio. Komori became the model for the character of Yamazaki Sōichi, the fixer, in Mishima's 1960 novel *After the Banquet* (Utage No Ato). In 1963 Komori was to choose his own candidate for the first time. His research institute was prospering, publishing a well-respected urban policy journal (*Tosei*), and his "graduates," bright young men who often came to him from Ōuchi's and Takahashi's economics seminars, were entering the Tokyo Metropolitan administration. He helped select Sakamoto Katsuo, a former governor of Hyogo prefecture, to run in Tokyo. This was Komori's third loss. It was still as much a conservative's paradise in Tokyo as it was nationwide.

9. See Minobe's personal account of Komori in the *Asahi Shimbun*, July 8, 1979.
10. Interview with former Tosei Chōsakai official (October 17, 1978) and Nippon Steel executive (November 24, 1978). See also Naitō (1975), Ch. 1.

But the chance that Komori had been waiting for presented itself to him in 1965, when a major bribery scandal involving more than a dozen LDP assembly members, including the assembly speaker, erupted in the Tokyo Metropolitan Assembly. Komori quickly moved to back a "committee of concerned citizens," all professors and prominent civic leaders, most of whom had been frequent contributors to *Tosei*, to act as a public voice in support of good government. This committee, together with the Socialists, Communists, Kōmeitō, Democratic Socialists, and most major labor organizations, helped organize a recall campaign which gained so much popular support that it precipitated the intervention of the national LDP which hurried a bill through the Diet dissolving the assembly. In the subsequent election the LDP tumbled from majority status to less than one-third of the seats. The Socialists now held a plurality, and Tokyo became the first major assembly to elect a progressive chief.

The stage was set in 1967 for Komori's fourth try at backing a leftist gubernatorial candidate. At the eleventh hour, due to the sudden withdrawal of Ōta Kaoru, the acknowledged frontrunner, Komori helped choose economics professor Minobe at the urging of Professors Ōuchi and Takahashi. Minobe had been a very popular and visible television personality, famous for his comprehensible explanations of economic problems and for his attacks upon the conservative central government. He was a good choice. In spite of the fact that Minobe had no administrative experience, he defeated two opponents to become only the third leftist-supported governor in Japan.[11]

From Komori's point of view, this lack of administrative experience was Minobe's greatest asset. By 1967 associates of Komori were in positions throughout the metropolitan government. Many of the "concerned citizens' committee," hand-picked by Komori, soon became key figures in the new Minobe administration. They headed his school board, civil service commission, pollution research center, and policy and planning office. Perhaps even more significant was the personal empire which Komori was creating among former Institute staffers who were now rising to division and department head posts within the

11. It should be noted that Komori's influence was by this time no longer restricted to Tokyo. He had spent much of the first decade of the Institute's existence traveling throughout Japan in support of progressive local government. He was still, at that time, a highly visible public figure. He was recognized as having an inexhaustible store of knowledge about urban policy problems (*Dokusho Shimbun*, March 30, 1964), and his "students" at the Institute were considered the best and brightest among Japan's many urban affairs specialists. His first victory was in fact not Minobe's but was the election of Shimano Takeshi in Sendai. Shimano, who was later to become with Yokohama mayor Asukata Ichio a leading figure in the National Association of Progressive Mayors, had been an attorney in the building next to Komori's Institute near Hibiya Park. It was Komori who reportedly first convinced Shimano to run, and it was Komori who reportedly bankrolled the effort.

metropolitan government's "nonpolitical" administrative hierarchy. By Minobe's second term Komori had created an environment inside the administration in which few moves could be taken either without his knowledge or his consent. He virtually controlled personnel movements within the administration. The Tokyo bureaucracy was said to be divided into Komori and anti-Komori factions, many of the latter resenting their role as *chabozu*, "tea servers to the Shōgun."

Komori had no authority but much power. He has variously been referred to as Minobe's "Rasputin," as his "Shadow Governor," as the "Hibiya Governor," and as the "master on the Tenth Floor" (jūkai no sensei). (This last is an allusion to the fact that there are only nine floors in the main offices of the Tokyo Metropolitan Government.) That Minobe did little without Komori was publicly acknowledged by Minobe after his retirement in 1979 when in a series of articles written for the *Asahi Shimbun* he noted that he had several daily phone conversations with Komori and that he met Komori at least once each week to map strategy. Minobe acknowledged that "on the whole, I followed Komori's opinions on political problems. There are not a few fine details and particulars about his behind the scenes maneuvering of which I know nothing" (*Asahi Shimbun*, July 7, 1979). In the following day's column, Minobe wrote: "The man who was what you might call my daily consultant, my most direct policy advisor, the man who played the most important role in the administration, was Komori Takeshi" (*Asahi Shimbun*, July 8, 1979). And he freely admits in personal conversation that "Komori was my man in the shadows for twelve years" (interview with Minobe Ryōkichi, September 20, 1979). Komori can be credited with everything from creating the famous slogan "Stop the Satō" in 1971, a slogan which punctuated the anticenter character of progressive local opposition, to such famous "Minobe" initiatives as the garbage war, the famous Tokyo antipollution policy, the Right to Sunshine policy, the abolition of public gambling, and other progressive programs. He is said to have prepared or at least to have initiated the preparation of all of Minobe's major public addresses. If Minobe was the star, Komori was the producer and director.

The Tokyo Bay General Development Council, created by Matsunaga and sacrificed to Komori's own calculus of political expediency, is but one case in point. The 1973 General Convention of the Council, at which the chairmanship passed from Minobe to Governor Tomono of Chiba, was held without incident in April. On July 4, Tokyo paid its annual dues to the Council secretariat. But only two days later, on July 6, Minobe dramatically announced at a press conference that Tokyo intended to withdraw from the Council. The decision had been Komori's.[12] By early June Komori had become concerned about the impending

---

12. The role of Komori in the Tokyo withdrawal is known only to a handful of those who were involved at the highest levels. The account which follows is based upon an interview with *Mainichi Shimbun* editor Naitō Kunio, a close associate of

prefectural assembly election scheduled for July 8. While the progressives (Socialists, Communists, and Kōmeitō) hoped to gain some seats (they already held a majority of 70 of the 125 seats), the LDP had hit upon a new and threatening strategy, a slogan calling for "the defense of a free society" which attacked the Minobe regime for its purported "left-wing socialism." In addition, now that the LDP was stepping on formerly progressive turf, by coopting much progressive rhetoric and policy, Komori feared at least the possibility of a reversal in favor of the LDP. He felt that without a dramatic display of progressive opposition the Minobe administration might lose the support of crucial independent voters. They could not afford to allow the right to coopt their most successful strategems, the anti-pollution and social service platforms. He needed to capture the imagination of the same voters who had been attracted to Minobe in the first place, voters who were voting as much for Minobe as against the central government. The withdrawal from the Council, announced two days before the election, and thus plastered across the front pages of the morning papers the day before polling took place, was orchestrated as a direct attack upon the center's growth policies, a maneuver which had paid off handsomely in previous elections.

This was politics as theater, staged and timed with exquisite attention to effect. It did not matter that Tokyo funds had been channeled through the Council to LDP coffers for the first six years of Minobe's administration. It did not matter that the cross-bay-bridge project had already been effectively frozen earlier in the year by the Tanaka government. It did not matter that Tokyo, through its Council membership, had been holding hands with industry throughout Minobe's tenure. It did not matter that Tokyo had never failed to endorse any of the Council's programs in the past and that Minobe had twice been Council chairman. Tokyo announced that it had a responsibility to oppose, and it chose election eve to demonstrate that responsibility. Whether for this reason or for others, the LDP lost four seats in a hotly contested election. The progressive majority coalition was returned to the assembly.

The political process behind the histrionics merits further attention for what it can teach us about the role of the political boss in Japan. What appeared publicly as a sudden and dramatic act was nothing of the sort. It was, however, a

Komori, who received a "leak" of the withdrawal intention in mid June, 1973. Throughout our interview (January 10, 1979), he referred to his notes from a conversation with Komori. The Komori role was later confirmed by two top Yokohama policy staffers under Asukata who had participated in the negotiations (interviews on April 3 and 6, 1979) and by a former director of the Tokyo Metropolitan Government Port and Harbor Authority (interview on January 31, 1979), who had received the withdrawal instructions. It was later reconfirmed to me on September 20, 1979, by former governor Minobe: "While both Komori and I had agreed upon the eventual necessity of withdrawing, it was he who picked the time and the circumstances. I went along with his decision at that time."

decision taken at the top, without consultation within the bureaucracy of the Tokyo Metropolitan Government. In particular, the working-level officials of the Port and Harbor Bureau, from whose budget the Council's dues were paid, had been very enthusiastic and active in the Council's activities. Minobe explains: "The top officials within my Port and Harbor Bureau, all products of previous administrations and not of my choosing, were not opposed to the Council or the bridge. That is why I had to rely so heavily upon Komori" (personal interview, September 20, 1979). The Port and Harbor people were not officially notified about the withdrawal until just before the action was taken, when they received on July 1 an internal memorandum (*ringisho*), with Governor Minobe's stamp affixed, entitled "Concerning the Withdrawal from the Tokyo Bay General Development Council." This memo involved no consultation, but merely contained a terse list of what were to become the publicly stated reasons for the withdrawal.[13] The notification came after Komori had already leaked the story to Naitō, his former associate and trusted editor of the *Mainichi Shimbun*. Naitō had published his report of the impending withdrawal as the lead article on page one of the June 20, 1973, evening edition. Feathers were understandably ruffled, and the Port and Harbor people cooperated only reluctantly with the policy.

If there was little or no consultation within the Tokyo bureaucracy, there was a great deal of it with the other member localities. Komori personally had telephone conversations in mid June with each of the other progressive chief executives of member localities. Although he was not necessarily seeking it, he received the assurances of each that the Tokyo withdrawal would be supported.[14] There is some question as to Komori's intentions vis-a-vis the role of these other progressive leaders. There is no evidence to suggest that he sought a joint withdrawal of the leftist localities, although such a possibility received extensive press treatment. This was enough for Komori, as the form, and not the substance, of a true progressive coalition was the objective in this case. Komori also reportedly contacted several of the banks which were members of the Council, as well as the conservative Chiba governor. The roots had been bound; power had been exercised from behind the throne.

13. A review of the internal memoranda concerning Tokyo's participation in the Council gives no indication that major policy decisions were ever initiated through the circulation of these documents. Contrary to Tsuji (1968) and others who see the *ringi seido* as a form of decision making from below, it seems that these memoranda are utilized only for communication of command decisions taken at the top on the one hand, or for the communication of the most routine sorts of activities, flagged for superiors by lower-ranking functionaries, on the other.
14. According to Naitō (interview January 10, 1979), much of the *nemawashi* was conducted by Komori *before* he even brought the idea to Minobe. The original discussions were conducted by Komori and several of his highly placed disciples in the administration.

Komori and Matsunaga had much in common besides enormous political power. Neither of them emerged from an established route within the bureaucracy, or even from the mainstream of the business community. Neither pursued purely personal gain. Both had something of the maverick in them and both were independent operators with great resources that transcended their personal influence with individual politicians. They accomplished things not only because of personal access to high-ranking public officials, but also because of a carefully constructed, broadly based, well-placed network of lower-ranking officials throughout a variety of public and private bureaucracies. It did not take long for "graduates" of Matsunaga's Industrial Planning Conference and of Komori's Metropolitan Policy Research Institute to ascend to positions of policy responsibility. Komori and Matsunaga were directors not only of elected officials, but also of the technicians who made their influence professional. It is both curious and instructive that neither was as widely known as many undistinguished politicians. Neither answered to an electorate, yet both had easy access to prime ministers and governors, to bankers and to cabinet ministers. Their differences were not stylistic: while Matsunaga was a godfather to the postwar, conservative power structure, Komori was one to the ascendent progressives.

The emphasis upon consensus in the secondary literature is not wrong, but it only covers part of the political phenomena involved. While it correctly posits the avoidance of conflict, it seems to assume that this results in open cooperation; to the extent that it does suggest the role of backstage politicking, it fails to systematically address the issues involved. This essay is therefore offered as an elaboration on the consensual model. Japanese men of power often remain fairly anonymous not because of the unstated dictates of consensual patterns of decision making, but because they are simply more effective out of the spotlight, free to nurture the connections which are the base of their power. While many of the most powerful political figures in Japan are by no means anonymous, the semianonymous *kuromaku* often play a decisive leadership role in shaping events, policies, and even the political climate more generally. Their power operates through networks of personal contacts and through organizations producing followers who can for years be mobilized when called upon. It is important to remember that *kuromaku* facilitate at least as much as they manipulate. Although they function more privately than do "charismatic" leaders in the West, they are nevertheless "great leaders" who clearly matter. This finding stands in contrast to many political studies, and stands in particular contrast to most studies of modern Japan.

References

Braden, Wythe Edward. 1979. Japanese leadership—a profile. *PHP* 10:27-64.

Caro, Robert A. 1974. *The power broker: Robert Moses and the fall of New York.* New York: Alfred A. Knopf.

Honda Yasuharu. 1975. Tōkyō no rasūpuchin: Komori Takeshi (Tokyo's Rasputin: Komori Takeshi). *Bungei Shunjū* June:278-90.

Hurst, G. Cameron. 1976. *Insei: Abdicated sovereigns in the politics of late Heian Japan, 1086-1185.* New York: Columbia University Press.

Ike Nobutaka. 1978. *A theory of Japanese democracy.* Boulder, Colorado: Westview Press.

Johnson, Chalmers. 1978. *Japan's public policy companies.* Washington, D.C.: American Enterprise Institute for Public Policy Research.

Komori Takeshi. 1966. Tochiji kōhosha senkō to shimin no tachiba (The people's position and the choice of a gubernatorial candidate for Tokyo). *Asahi Jānaru,* September 4, p. 20-25.

Lasswell, Harold D., and Abraham Kaplan. 1950. *Power and society.* New Haven: Yale University Press.

Matsuyama Yoshimitsu. 1978. Tosei no don Komori Takeshi no tsugi no sakubō (The next strategem of the don of Tokyo's administration, Komori Takeshi). *Gendai* August:236-42.

Naitō Kunio. 1975. *Minobe tosei no sugao* (The unpainted face of the Minobe administration). Tokyo: Kōdansha.

Nakane Chie. 1970. *Japanese society.* Berkeley: University of California Press.

Otani Ken. 1978. *Kōbō: denryoku o meguru seiji to keizai* (The politics and economics of the changing fortunes of the electric power industry). Tokyo: Sangyō Nōritsu Tanki Daigaku Shuppansha.

Reischauer, Edwin O. 1977. *The Japanese.* Cambridge: Harvard University Press.

Samuels, Richard J. 1982. *The Politics of Regional Policy in Japan: Localities Incorporated?* Princeton: Princeton University Press.

Scott, James C. 1972. *Comparative political corruption.* Englewood Cliffs, New Jersey: Prentice Hall.

Tarrow, Sidney. 1977. *Between center and periphery: grassroots politicians in Italy and France.* New Haven: Yale University Press.

Thayer, Nathaniel. 1969. *How the conservatives rule Japan.* Princeton: Princeton University Press.

Tsuji, Kiyoaki. 1968. Decision-making in the Japanese government: a study of
    ringi-sei. In R. E. Ward, ed., *Political development in modern Japan*.
    Princeton: Princeton University Press.

Yoshino, Michael Y. 1968. *Japan's managerial system*. Cambridge: M.I.T. Press.

CONTRIBUTORS

Kent E. Calder studied at Harvard, where he is a research associate, and is coauthor of *The Eastasia Edge*.

Susan J. Pharr studied at Columbia and is associate professor of political science at the University of Wisconsin. She wrote *Women in Japanese Politics*.

Terry Edward MacDougall's degree is from Yale; he is associate professor of government at Harvard. His forthcoming book is *Localism and Political Opposition in Japan*.

Ellis S. Krauss studied at Stanford and is associate professor of political science at Western Washington University. Recently, he coedited *Political Opposition and Local Politics in Japan* and the forthcoming *Conflict in Japan*.

Ronald Aqua, who studied at Cornell, is a staff associate in charge of Japanese and Korean studies at the Social Science Research Council.

Richard J. Samuels studied and is now assistant professor of political science at MIT. His *The Politics of Regional Policy in Japan: Localities Incorporated?* will appear soon.

MICHIGAN PAPERS IN JAPANESE STUDIES

No. 1. *Political Leadership in Contemporary Japan*, edited by Terry Edward MacDougall.

No. 2. *Parties, Candidates and Voters in Japan; Six Quantitative Studies*, edited by John Creighton Campbell.

No. 3. *The Japanese Automobile Industry: Model and Challenge for the Future?*, edited by Robert E. Cole.

No. 4. *Survey of Japanese Collections in the United States, 1979-1980*, by Naomi Fukuda.

No. 5. *Culture and Religion in Japanese-American Relations: Essays on Uchimura Kanzō, 1861-1930*, edited by Ray A. Moore.

No. 6. *Sukeroku's Double Identity: The Dramatic Structure of Edo Kabuki*, by Barbara E. Thornbury.

No. 7. *Industry at the Crossroads*, edited by Robert E. Cole.

No. 8. *Treelike: The Poetry of Kinoshita Yūji*, translated by Robert Epp.